FINDING HOPE

Finding Hope

A BIRTHMOTHER'S JOURNEY
INTO THE LIGHT

Hope O Baker

LIONCREST
PUBLISHING

FINDING HOPE
A Birthmother's Journey into the Light

ISBN   978-1-5445-0486-5 *Paperback*
      978-1-5445-0487-2 *Ebook*
      978-1-5445-0488-9 *Audiobook*

To my beautiful son, I loved you then, I love you now, and I will love you always.

For all of the women and men out there who are going through a hard time, I believe in your pain and in your strength. We can all do this. We will find our light.

—Hopey

Contents

Note: In the following pages, some names have been changed.

Introduction

This past Christmas, for the first time in six years, I didn't need to take a break to cry alone, slumped in a sobby mess on some cold bathroom floor.

It was the first time I could say that about a holiday—*any* holiday—in all that time. The years since my son was born. The years since I placed him for adoption.

This year, I wasn't bawling. I was baking.

Cupcakes, actually. And wearing an apron, even. The whole bit.

As I stood at the sink, I looked out at the commotion going on in my home. There was my fiancée, the man I love. There were my stepkids, causing a ruckus. I was surrounded by friends, too. It was crazy, but a good crazy.

My crazy.

For the first time in a long time, on a day that was supposed to be a celebration, I could actually celebrate. I could be present. I didn't feel like I needed to self-medicate or go ugly cry in the bathroom—at least not the whole time. I knew I would see my son soon, on my upcoming visit.

And you know what? I felt it, then—something warming, something a long time coming: I was okay.

But I wasn't always.

A LONG ROAD

At twenty-one years old, I placed my son for adoption. I opted for the open route, and I met (and even lived with) my son's adoptive mother before he was born. I knew it was the right decision for my son's life at the time, even if it didn't feel best for mine. I did it for him.

As mothers, that's what we do, right? We make the best decisions we can for our children, even if those decisions break us.

And let me tell you, I was fucking broken. Over and over again, a little more every day. We'll get to that later.

Even today, after a long journey of finding my way back to the light, I'm still not all the way healed. Yes, I have a wonderful fiancé and beautiful stepkids who fill my days with love. Yes, I love my family and friends. Yes, I am successful professionally. Yes, I have found a way to love myself again. Yes, I get to see my son on our scheduled visits, and that time together is more precious than gold. And yes, he is thriving with his adoptive mother—someone so perfect for my son, someone who is a wonderful mother to my son.

I'm better than I was during all those on-the-floor Christmases and better than I was during my downward spiral into depression and addiction. I'm blooming now, again. My fiancée and I have even discussed the potential of having a child of our own—a complicated decision I'll cover later in this book. There are many considerations: How would my son feel if I did that? Will I ever be able to show him that he was always enough for me, but I wasn't always enough for him?

Time will tell. In the meantime, I'm still moving forward into possibility. Into Hope. It's been a long road, and I'm still on it.

If you're reading this, you're likely on a long road of your own. I'm here to walk with you.

YOUR PAIN IS YOUR PAIN

If you're a birthmother, I want you to know that I see you. It's the worst pain you've ever felt, right? Living and existing in a completely separate world from your child? You can't hug or kiss them. You can't smell them. You can't cheer them on from the sidelines. Maybe you feel like a vessel—an empty one, when it's all said and done. I know I did.

I've been on the other side of the story, too. I got pregnant in high school, even though I was on the Depo shot. I found out at nine weeks. I remember getting sick at school and having my mom come pick me up. (Turns out it was morning sickness.) She drove me to a Walgreens and we bought a pregnancy test. While we waited for the results, I sobbed. *How did this happen? I'm on birth control,* I wondered.

After we saw a positive result, we drove to Fargo, North Dakota, to get an abortion. I remember protestors at the clinic. I remember having to stand before a judge and say why I wanted an abortion—a required act when both parents weren't present to consent to the procedure for a minor, and my dad wasn't there. I remember sitting in the little waiting room, reading letters other women who'd also gotten abortions had written. I remember having a couple emotional breakdowns in the car on the way home. I remember being in pain.

But it was the right choice. All that's to say that I am not writing this book about being a birthmother because I'm anti-abortion. I'm not. I want to make the point that pain is pain. I've seen it everywhere, including watching my mom and sister suffer miscarriage after miscarriage.

But there's light through all that pain, too, even if it's hard to see sometimes. And I'm writing this book because I want you to know that you deserve good things in life, too, even though it can be hard to see right now. I know where you've been: to hell. The deepest hell, because it was one you had to consciously *choose*. Whether that was out of love for your child or an understanding of your circumstances or both—that's no matter. What matters is that you went down a path you knew would be covered in thorns, and you stepped out onto it anyway. You bled. You did what you had to do.

Maybe you're not a birthmother. Maybe you're an adoptive parent. Maybe you chose to keep your child and raise them on your own. Maybe you chose to have an abortion. Again, no matter. Your choices are your choices—as a mother and as a human—and I respect your right to make them. I'm not saying my path is the only path, by any means, but it *was* mine. This is my story, and I want to use my voice to tell it in the hope I can reach more women who are struggling. My message is simple: *you are not alone.*

The subtitle of this book is *A Birthmother's Journey Into the Light* for a reason. It is a journey. I still have bad days. I still fall down. My pain is my pain, just like your pain is your pain, no matter where it comes from. You are entitled to feel it, to grieve. To crumble on *your* bathroom floor if you need to. Or any floor. You're allowed to take up space in this world.

This shit hurts. Let it. Slowly, you can start to let light in little by little. I'm proof that getting there won't be perfect, but it's possible.

WHAT'S NEXT?

In this book, I will share my journey—all the pieces— authentically and without reservation. And let me tell you right now, it isn't always pretty. (I haven't been baking cupcakes all these years.)

In the end, I'm writing this book as a woman hoping to empower other women. I'm writing this book to help you if you find yourself in a similar position. Looking back, if I spoke about my feelings and felt supported enough to reach out in those rough moments, maybe I wouldn't have felt so alone. I wish I wouldn't have gone through those years of having to get high or drunk to talk about my son, of self-destructing because I didn't know what else to do. I can't go back in time, but I can go forward. And along the way, I can spread this message of Hope.

This is a story of my brokenness, and this is a story of my healing. This is a story that shows *birthmother* isn't a dirty word. This is a story that shows adoption can be messy, but also that it can be beautiful. This is a story that says *whatever* choice you make, that's okay; you are still worthy of love. I will stand by you.

You walked this path for your child, as I did for mine. Mostly, this book is a love letter to my son.

CHAPTER ONE

♥

An Unexpected Pregnancy

"You're pregnant," the nurse told me, her voice soft. Like she was walking on eggshells. Like she knew what she said might break me, even before she said it. I couldn't look at her.

I'd come to the clinic because I knew I wasn't feeling well. Something wasn't right, and I'd been trying to figure it out for weeks, months maybe. I'd gone to two different clinics, but never once had anyone tested my urine for pregnancy. I hadn't thought to, either, because of my medical history. I'd been on the Depo shot in the past, which had stopped my periods. I just didn't think of being pregnant.

Neither did the doctors, apparently. In fact, they gave me a CT scan in the beginning of my pregnancy, but ultimately they said I was probably paranoid given my mom's diagnosis. They called it phantom pain. Eventually, they treated me for a severe urinary tract infection, mostly, but it wasn't helping. I'd just returned from an x-ray, as the doctor was trying to determine the cause of my symptoms. My mother—who had just been diagnosed with breast cancer and was fighting her own battles—sat in a different room to wait, likely fearing the worst.

Instead of a tumor, though, they found a baby.

Pregnant? I thought. *What? I'd never thought that was possible.*

I remember laying back on the cold bed, looking at everything around me. From that angle, it all seemed so tall, so out of reach.

"Wait, what?" I asked, this time aloud.

"The x-ray technician who did your procedure saw a skeleton on the scan," she said. "And we've now tested your urine. It's positive for pregnancy."

A skeleton? I can't believe they used that word.

"Where is my mom?" I managed to choke out between tears as I rocked back and forth in the bed, cradling myself. "What are my options?"

I repeated those two questions over and over. They were the only words I had.

TROUBLE IN ALEXANDRIA

When I found out I was pregnant, I was twenty-one years old and in college. I didn't think kids were ever part of my plan. I always wanted to be the "cool aunt." I had no clue what to do. Disbelief and shock rocked me to my core.

Before finding the skeleton—which still bothers me, to this day, that they worded it that way—the doctor had me on an IV because my kidneys were failing. As soon as they discovered I was pregnant, the nurse rushed to switch the medication in the drip.

The nursing staff quickly sent me down for an ultrasound. Upon arrival, the technician spoke to me about God during the entire examination. I was crying uncontrollably, unable to look at the screen, as she continued to explain that this situation was a gift. She told me stories about her son, who was once "living in sin" and had gotten his girlfriend pregnant. She went on to tell me they'd gotten married, had the baby, and done "the right thing." Throughout the examination, she'd stop every so often to cry and tell me point blank that this was one of God's children, and this baby was God's gift to me.

I didn't know I needed to be saved.

I *did* know I had just learned I was over twenty weeks pregnant. Yes, twenty.

I was vulnerable, still in shock, and would have given anything to get out of that room with that woman. The woman I *wanted* was my mother, who had been told I was moved to ultrasound, but not why—likely making her fear that I had cancer all the more real. I asked if she could be in the room with me while a nurse explained the situation. I wanted us all to be there together so everything could be clear.

That didn't happen.

When I finally made it back to my room and my mom walked in, I didn't have to tell her the news. The nurses already had, against my wishes.

My mom looked at me then, and I could see her heart break for me. There's this face my mom makes when she's going to cry but is holding it back, and she made that face then. She held my hand, acting as my advocate. She said we would look at all our options and make an educated decision based on the information we had. All we wanted was more information. We both asked a version of "What are my options" at least eight times, but the nurse and the OB doctor on call only answered with statements like, "You're halfway done," or "There are people out there who would want this child."

I couldn't stop shaking. My mom was getting pissed.

The nurse and doctor left us alone for a moment, then returned to the room with news: there was an employee in their clinic who wanted to meet me immediately. She was interested in adopting my child "no matter what mental issues and deformities the baby might have because of my lack of prenatal care for the first half of my pregnancy."

I remember that direct quote with my whole being. Yes, they said that.

Wait, would my baby even be okay? Was he hurt? I had a whole new set of worries. I couldn't breathe.

The doctor then said I should be checked in to the hospital immediately to be started on medicine and receive prenatal care. She added that a social worker would come talk to me about adoption—which I'd never once requested. My mom saw the look of fear and hurt on my face. The Christian rhetoric, the over-the-top language, the refusal to answer my questions, the stranger who wanted to adopt my baby two hours after I found out I was carrying him—it was too much. I had to get out of there.

We left then, against medical advice, and agreed to come back the following day to follow up because I was, after all, still very sick. It was a risk not to go to the hospital as advised, but I didn't want to be trapped or persecuted more. That night, my mom took care of me. Together, we researched the options they wouldn't tell me about in the office. We made calls, even reaching out to organizations to help with costs associated with not only the abortion, but travel, etc. I needed the help because, even though my parents supported the abortion, they weren't going to pay for it. And, as a poor college student, I didn't have piles of money laying around.

That night, my mom and I found so many resources and so much support. We learned there was a clinic in Kansas City that would perform abortions past twenty weeks, and we decided I would go there. I felt then that I just couldn't do it. I couldn't have a baby. In truth, I was still reeling from the events of the past twenty-four hours.

In the morning, I debated going back to the clinic in Alexandria. I didn't want to, but I wasn't sure what else to do. I was so ill that my skin was turning gray, and I needed my medical records to take to Kansas City. When I checked in, the nurse who wanted to adopt my baby stood behind the counter—a skinny woman with long, dark straight hair. She was waiting for me. We looked at one another, but never spoke.

You've got to be fucking kidding me, I thought.

I walked to the OB-GYN side of the clinic and checked in. When my mom and I met with the doctor, we explained we'd done our research and that I'd be going to Kansas City to get an abortion. The doctor urged me not to and said it wasn't right. My mom and I knew we were within a couple days of the cutoff to be eligible for an abortion— and the doctor must have known that too, because the dates she included on my forms made it appear I was further along and thus ineligible for the procedure.

Even though so much was up in the air, I was never fuzzy on the dates. I didn't know what to do next, but I of course knew exactly how it happened. My son was conceived when I was twenty. It was a Christmas party. A drunken night. A college, one-time thing. Both sides made mistakes. There's nothing more to say about it, other than I was sure of the date more than I was sure of anything else in that moment. The day after it happened, I drove home and learned my mom had cancer, and I wasn't sexually active after that. There was no doubt in my mind.

My mom and I had to ask the doctor to rewrite the dates on the forms to prove how far along I *really* was—which she did, after a struggle. Eventually, she scribbled out the falsified dates while pleading with my mother to make me reconsider, as if it were her choice and not mine.

It took a concerted effort between my mom and I to get the records. The clinic kept telling us they weren't ready, or they couldn't find them, etc. After arguing, we finally got the papers. When we picked up the ultrasound picture, I couldn't look.

I left the clinic in Alexandria and never went back.

TO THE ABORTION CLINIC AND BACK AGAIN

My mom and I started the drive to Kansas City immediately. On the road, she got a call from the Mayo Clinic saying she was cleared for her hysterectomy—a surgery she'd been waiting on—so we had to turn around. When we got to Mayo, I got very ill. I had to tell them I was pregnant, and they gave me fluids. My sister, Amber, met us there. I didn't have much time, so Amber dropped everything—literally, she left work and got in her car—to help me get to Kansas City.

I don't remember the car ride. I don't remember what I was thinking or feeling. I think I blocked it out. Looking back, I wonder what my mom must have felt like then: I was exercising my reproductive rights while she was losing hers.

My next memory is being in the hotel that night. We'd used my mom's points to book the room, and I recall emailing my college professors to ask for extensions on my finals. I took one final that night, too. Everything else is a blur.

It's funny, really—what you remember and what you don't when your mind is trying to protect you. Except it's not really funny at all. Not even a little.

The next day, we went to the clinic. The doctor there was kind and supportive. My memories here come in snippets. I can still hear the voices of the staff...

"It'll be cutting it close. You may need to go to New Mexico, where they perform abortions a little later."

"You're right on the line. It might be touchy."

"This is your choice. Is anybody pressuring you to do this?"

"Whatever you decide, we're here for you."

At one point, I looked up at my sister. We locked watery eyes. I knew it, and she knew it: I couldn't go through with it. I just couldn't. She knew my face. She knew she needed to get me out of there.

When the doctor said it would be touchy, I felt relief. Maybe in my head, I was looking for a reason for it not to work out—but not because I thought I wanted to keep the baby. I didn't. I was so confused: I knew I couldn't have the baby, but I didn't want to abort the baby, either. To this day, my strongest memory of that clinic was telling my sister, "Get me out of here."

After we checked out of the hotel room and started our drive back to Minnesota, my sister and I stopped at a gas station. We'd been driving for a while, and we'd been eating chips and snacks we'd packed for the road. I had a tight shirt on. As we got out of the car, I think I just let go. I stopped sucking my stomach in. I'd known I was pregnant for almost a week at that point, but I never let myself *feel* it until that moment. Everything had been too traumatic.

In that moment, I looked at my belly—my damn near four-month pregnant belly—and thought, *Holy shit. This is real.* I know my sister saw it, too. We both smiled. I hadn't smiled in a while.

We faced a difficult conversation for the remainder of our trip. At the time, Amber was trying to get pregnant, and she and her husband were having fertility problems. She offered to adopt the baby, but we didn't know how it would all work. Would she give him back when I was ready? Would I be an aunt? A mom? How weird would that be at Thanksgiving? What would that look like? We decided that for our situation, it was best if we didn't pursue that option. Amber said she'd stay in my corner no matter what, and she's never wavered.

FOR A REASON

Looking back, I'd gotten pregnant at the perfect time for my life situation. Before that, I was a typical college student—drinking, smoking, and partying, as people do. Then, my mom was diagnosed with breast cancer, and a switch flipped. I started to mother my own mother. I had to. The need to be there was fierce within me.

It was interesting because my mom and I always had a hard relationship. When she got sick, we were in a rocky place. There were times before that when we wouldn't speak for months because we'd gotten into a blowout argument. Still, when she was diagnosed, I couldn't imagine not being there for her. It was instinctual.

I went into full-on caretaker mode, driving from Minneapolis to Alexandria, Minnesota, where my mom and stepdad lived, regularly. I was there to help care for my little brother, who was and still is a shining star in my life. And, of course, for my mother, who underwent twelve surgeries over the course of her treatment. After her double mastectomy, I remember separating her pills, laboring over the medication schedule to make sure I got it right, and setting alarms to administer the meds in enough time to ensure she didn't wake up in pain.

Taking care of my mother consumed me. Internally, I knew what I wanted was more time with her. More time to be close. More time to have a mother. More time to be a daughter. I almost took an entire semester off school because I got so far behind during that time, and I was grateful that the professors really worked with me. I got so much support from them and even the president of the school. It was touching.

During that time, I also battled anxiety over my own health, working out and striving to eat healthy to avoid the risk of cancer in my own body. In reality, my own body was working on something of its own that whole time: growing a baby. My beautiful boy.

My mom getting cancer was one of the hardest things I'd ever had to deal with at the time, but looking back, we both agree it was a blessing in disguise. We had all these experiences for a reason. My son is here for a reason.

"YOU'RE NOT KEEPING IT, RIGHT?"

I'd gone to Kansas City pregnant, and I was leaving Kansas City—still pregnant. I had people to call.

As Amber drove, I dialed. I called my mom, telling her I'd gotten to see the baby and couldn't do it. She said she'd help me get to another abortion clinic that would do late-term abortions in New Mexico, if that's what I wanted to do. She said she'd support me either way.

I called my girlfriend Jill, who'd just had a baby. I called my dad, who said I could move in with him and offered to turn one of his bedrooms into a nursery. I called my other sister, Abby, who was so excited that I'd be the first of my siblings to have a baby. I kept calling those close to me as the miles passed, trying to get feedback. Trying to make it more real the more I said it aloud. Looking back, I wonder how my sister felt, listening to those conversations while she was struggling so hard to conceive herself.

When I got back to Minnesota, I was still unsure what I was going to do. I met up with Jill—who brought her baby along—and my best friend, Bethany. We went to get shakes, and I spilled the news. Bethany's reaction stuck with me:

"You're not keeping it, right?"

It was completely reactive. Bethany had known me for years. Ultimately, I knew she'd support me no matter what, and I don't blame her for responding that way.

I got similar reactions from others, too.

When my dad pitched the idea of moving in with him—in his tiny, conservative Iowa town—I thought that sounded absolutely miserable. There's nothing wrong with that sort of place; it's just never been my ideal home. Plus, he was having challenges of his own with drugs. It was only five years later, when my sister called me, that I'd learn he had been arrested for meth. All I knew at the time, though, was that I felt like he'd abandoned me—I didn't know he was fighting his own demons. I declined the invitation, and we didn't talk for a long time after that.

Once, when I was still making up my mind, I went to Target. Among other items, I bought a soft baby blanket. When I showed my mom, she was pissed—*very* pissed. We stood on the staircase in her house, five stairs apart, arguing.

"Hope, you can't do this," she screamed. "You are *not* going to be a good mother."

I've blocked out a lot, but I can never block that out—even though, sometimes, I think I want to.

Whatever decision I was going to make didn't matter then, because what my mother said is what I believed. Her approach wasn't the best, but in the end, she didn't want me to get hurt.

That comment solidified it: I wouldn't be a good mother. From that moment on, I never looked back. Adoption it was.

CHAPTER TWO

♥

Meeting My Son's Mom

As I began to navigate the adoption waters, I pursued a couple of different options. My sister knew a couple in Iowa who wanted to adopt. I had several conversations with them, but it never felt right. They were too close to home, and it wasn't clicking. I spoke to a gay couple from New York City who seemed like lovely people, but it didn't click, either. I also registered online with adoption agencies—and let me tell you, they were on their game. I registered one day, and the next day, a packet showed up at my door. In my research, I saw the adoption "books" for many couples—the packages hopeful adoptive parents put together that tell their stories. It tells you who they are, what kind of parents they'll be, and why they're seeking adoption.

One evening, I was sitting in a recliner upstairs at my

mom's house, watching television and searching on Google. I'd already read thousands of adoption books from prospective parents.

Then, I saw it, there on the side of the page like an ad: an adoption book that would change my life, and my son's life, forever.

Holy shit, I thought. *This is it.*

I just *knew*. As I read more, I learned this adoptive mother lived in California. She wanted to be a mother more than anything—something she'd decided later in life—and wanted to do that as a single parent by choice. She had her life together and wasn't on anyone else's timeline. She wanted to do this and knew she was capable! I could tell she was very in tune with herself. *This is who I want to be someday*, I thought. *This is the kind of life I want my child to have.*

I didn't even know the woman, but I had a warm, comfortable feeling as I reviewed her adoption book. We even looked alike, in a way. I emailed her to reach out (and also her lawyer, to make sure she was a legit person) and I felt my son kicking in my belly—just more proof that it was all for a reason.

After emailing and texting back and forth for a short time,

we decided to video chat via Skype. My mom met her, too, that way. My mom had thought the adoption book was fake and had hoped I didn't see it, but I did. In fact, the more this woman and I talked, the more I wanted to pursue her as my baby's adoptive parent. I looked up to her instantly, and I never even searched again for another placement option after her ad came up on Google. We'd only communicated using technology at that point, but I already couldn't imagine breaking her heart.

About two weeks after that fateful Google search, I was on a plane out to California to meet the woman who would become my son's adoptive mother.

THE "HOLY GRAIL"

I saw her as soon as I stepped into the baggage claim in the Los Angeles Airport. She was (and is) beautiful without trying to be, dressed in solid colors and exuding confidence and approachability at the same time. Although I anticipated being nervous or scared, I wasn't.

We went to dinner that night at a small Italian place, and I wanted to order spaghetti—my favorite meal. There was one problem: the menu said spaghetti Bolognese, something I'd never heard before, being from the Midwest. She explained it patiently, and we shared a laugh. Even today, I can see her in her car on the way home, her arm resting on the console as we discussed plans for the next day.

The next day, she got me a prenatal massage. Then, we went to the beach, and she brought her friend along. Both their dogs came with us—Sadie and Koda. We picked up sandwiches and packed the car together. From those early moments, she included me in her life, and meeting her friends gave me a better sense of who she was as a person. I'd never been to California, so putting on sunscreen at the beach didn't cross my mind. I got a terrible burn that day; I didn't know the sun could be that different.

That day at the beach, I wasn't just meeting my son's mother, but I was also meeting the life my son would have. I envisioned it—these would be his sandwiches, his ocean days.

My son's mother also told me her dad owned a couple McDonald's, and we joked that the baby would have chicken nuggets for life—funny, because I loved chicken nuggets. This made me feel warm.

That night, we ordered in from the best Chinese restaurant ever. (My mother and I would end up going back to this same place two days after my son was born, although we obviously didn't know how full-circle it all would come then.) The more I got to know the woman who would become my son's mother, the more I fell in love with the idea of my baby growing up with her and me being a part of his life in some way. I still wasn't sure how much contact I wanted, but we both agreed we wanted the baby to know where he came from. It was an open adoption from day one—we just needed to sort out the details. I knew I wanted to be far away because being too close seemed too hard—an intuition that would prove very true later on. I just wasn't sure what it all would look like.

As this was our initial meeting, we were still feeling each other out, to a degree. I knew that I was, as both my lawyer and her lawyer would eventually tell me, the "holy grail" of birthmothers. I came from a good family, was educated, did not have problems with health, and had full-coverage health insurance. In those early moments in California, though, I felt like I'd found the holy grail of an adoptive parent for my son. Some people are picky when it comes to adoption, wanting particular genders or races. She was the opposite; she didn't care. Although she hadn't been looking long, she told me I was not the first birthmother she talked to, and she expressed that she did feel lucky to have found me. In that moment, I felt the same about her.

THE FATHER, FALTERING

My son's father and I hadn't had much communication

since he'd gotten the news I was pregnant, and what little communication we did have was not positive. First, he immediately told me to get an abortion and that the baby wasn't his. Then, when I didn't get an abortion, he went back and forth—he said he was going to help a little, then he said he was not going to help at all. It was a toss-up, and I wasn't betting on a toss-up. I didn't even want to. It never crossed my mind to try to be with him.

When I boarded the flight home from LA, I remember eating chicken nuggets and getting texts from him. I told him I'd met the woman who would become my son's mother, he started to flex a little more, and his messages became more demanding. He began to say he had the power. He said if I placed my son, he still got to name him. And he refused or neglected to sign contracts, saying he'd lost them or couldn't get them notarized. It became abusive and stressful, and eventually he was issued a no-contact with me. We weren't allowed to connect.

After the attorneys explained he'd need to pay for the baby for the first eighteen years of his life, he changed his tune and signed—although that took a while to get to, and I'd be living in LA by the time it was all said and done.

A HELLO, A GOODBYE—FOR NOW

Driving back from dinner with her—after a day at the

beach where I'd gotten fried in the California sun—she mentioned a beautiful, trendy hotel she'd like me to see in West Hollywood: Chateau Marmont.

"I'll take you there if you come back," she said, as we sat in traffic in the rare shade of a Los Angeles underpass.

"I'll be back," I told her, knowing it in that moment. And I meant it.

She grabbed my hand. That moment was our way of saying, *Let's do this together.*

And we did—but first, I'd have to get out of Minnesota.

CHAPTER THREE

♥

A Life-Changing Move

Working at the Arrowwood Deck Bar back in Alexandria, Minnesota, was a coveted job, as it was frequented by tourists and often felt like a big party. I'd spent previous summers there, working and hanging out. It was right on the water, and the servers and bartenders made a killing.

I was one of them. But the difference was that I was wearing my bright green shirt and apron to hide my growing belly.

I'd recently come back from California, visiting the woman who would become my son's mother, and I needed to bank some money. Because I paid my own way through college, I was always working. Always the last one to leave. I'd work my closing shifts—those were the ones I wanted, because I could say I was too tired to go out with my friends so they wouldn't suspect anything—then go straight to the ATM to deposit what I'd earned. That money had a purpose: to go toward my credit cards and expenses I knew I might have soon.

I only told two people at Arrowwood that I was pregnant: my friend Karen and my shift manager, Cheryl. When we were walking in to set up the deck bar, Karen was talking about how she was excited to party all summer. I had to break the news to her then that I wouldn't be joining her—I was pregnant. She was in disbelief, as we'd both gotten the job nailed down months before. Even though she was in shock, she told me she'd help with whatever I needed. As for Cheryl, it turned out she was looking to adopt a baby; it was like I couldn't get away from it, but she never pressured me one bit. They both supported me and said they'd help out whenever they could.

One shift, though, it all became too much. It was the Fourth of July, and I was fucking miserable. My feet and legs were swollen, and I just couldn't do it anymore. The heat. The running food back and forth to boats. The pouring drinks. The hours and hours of standing.

Prior to that, my mom and little brother had come in to eat. They sat at the bar with me, and she couldn't understand why the young servers wouldn't run food down to boats for me. I told her it was because they didn't know I was pregnant. That's why I was still switching kegs, stocking shelves, etc. My mom even offered to take the food down for me. In the end, my little brother, Riley, did it.

It wasn't just at work that nobody knew. Few people knew in my personal life. I remember a dramatic moment when I walked into the clinic for my glucose test, and I was shocked when my friend's mom was the nurse who would be administering it. She was positive and encouraging, promising me she wouldn't say anything to her daughter. It was the opposite of my experience in the other clinic in Alexandria.

That summer, I wasn't lying when I told my friends I couldn't go out with them: I wasn't just tired. I was exhausted. I was living with my mom and stepdad, but even being surrounded by people, I often felt so alone. Nobody understood.

After a fourteen-hour day on the Fourth of July at the deck bar, I was done.

I can never come back here, I thought. *I can't do it anymore. How is this affecting my son in there? In this heat? Is he okay?*

I had been in conversation with my son's mother before then about moving. I'd had talks with my mom, too. I just knew I couldn't be there anymore. My mom suggested

I go live with my grandma, but my poor grandmother didn't even know I was pregnant. So many people didn't know. My son's mother's attorney suggested I go live in a maternity home in Texas—something that broke my heart. And, to her credit, she made sure I never had to speak to that particular attorney again. I don't know if it was hormones or reality—a bit of both—but that attorney treated me like a piece of trash. That was odd, since I was growing a baby inside my body.

One day, during one of our normal discussions, my son's mother suggested I come live with her in California, as I remember it. We had legal questions to answer, of course, but as for the logistics of the decision, it all clicked in that moment. I'd been telling her about every doctor's appointment, sending her ultrasound pictures—everything. My family, too, knew what we'd been discussing (all except for my little brother).

When I presented the idea of the move to them, they had mixed reactions about my upcoming life change. I had just over eight weeks left in my pregnancy, and I'd lost many people in my life. My sister Abby and I weren't talking due to a misunderstanding. I wasn't speaking with my older brother about it because our relationship was already unpredictable. My father also wasn't talking to me, as he was still pissed I'd declined his offer to move into his house—a decision that was a positive in my mind.

My mom and I also had a toxic relationship at the time—
good one moment, then we'd set each other off the next.
We both contributed to that environment—the stress of
which was not good on me or the baby.

My sister Amber was supportive of my decision, and so
was my stepfather—a man who walked into my life when
I was eight and chose to be a parent to me and my three
siblings. I still remember the first time we met: I was eight,
and it was my first communion. He, a Canadian, brought
me and my brother hockey skates. I wanted to be his best
buddy from the very beginning.

He was incredible then and still is now, always saying he
didn't want me or the baby to get hurt. In fact, he'd seen
the consequences of the negative side of birthmother situations: he knew someone who'd gotten pregnant out of
wedlock at a young age, and she was sent to a religious
compound. It was a different time. Her child was born
deaf, and she was never able to find the baby again. It
tormented her, and he'd seen the pain she struggled with
as an adult. He didn't want that for me.

It was always going to be an open adoption. Ours would
just start a little differently, because I was about to move
across the country.

The weekend before I moved to my son's mother's house

was my stepdad's work banquet. It was an annual event for us. I switched plane tickets so I could spend that last weekend with my family. It felt like a goodbye. Amber and her husband were there, and Amber was the one who dropped me off at the airport in the end.

Eleven days after my last shift at the deck bar, I moved in with my son's mother in Los Angeles. The point was that I wanted to bring my son into a situation where I knew his new family would not only love him and take care of him, but wouldn't be strangers to him. Or to me. Plus, I wanted her to experience the pregnancy, too.

A NEW LIFE IN LA

As soon as I got off the plane, I went straight to my attorney's office. We'd been talking via phone and email, but we needed to meet in person to discuss process and paperwork. My son's mother and I had agreed that she would pay my bills while I was there and for two months after I gave birth. We had also agreed I would get a $200 per week stipend to live on, which is standard in adoption in some states. I was lucky that she lived in California, where birthmothers have some rights; in some states, they don't have as many.

The assistance with bills was important to me because I fully supported myself. It took a while, I think, for her to understand that, as she'd had support from her parents while she was in school. Once, when we went to see the movie *Blackfish* with her family, I remember commenting on how expensive something was, and we actually had a conversation about why I needed the financial support while there. It was a watershed moment; I felt like she understood me more then. That same morning, her family had wanted to walk to the movie after eating breakfast. With one look at my face, she could tell I didn't want to walk, and she said we would drive. She just *got me* like that sometimes.

There were many times while living in LA that she went out of her way to understand and support me, too. She taught me how to use Uber. She'd ask me what I was craving. Once, when I said "wedding cake," we laughed before setting out to find a wedding-cake flavored cupcake. We'd lay on the floor for hours and watch *Orange Is the New Black*. We walked the dog every day. While she was at work, I'd stay home—very pregnant—or walk to the mall. When she got home, she'd often ask if I wanted to go to my favorite cookie spot, Magnolia's. Sometimes I'd go to Magnolia's during the day, and she'd ask if I wanted to go when she got home from work. I always said yes!

At all times, she wanted me to be fed, happy, and comfortable.

Once when she was at work, I heard a knock at the door. Because she lived in West Hollywood, she had many friends who were in the music or television industry, and it turned out to be one of those friends.

Oh shit, I thought. *Do I answer?*

The woman outside saw me, so I opened the door. Her friend was funny, beautiful, and pleasant—just stopping by to say hello. She looked over to see a popular television show playing, and she saw her husband on the screen! It was surreal.

"Oh my God," she said before she left. "Why is it so hot in here?"

"It is hot, yeah," I said. "But I feel bad turning the air on."

"Oh, honey," she said. "Don't worry about it. Turn the damn air on."

She was right. And her friends would do anything for anybody, too. One of her other friends knew my favorite show was *Grey's Anatomy*, so she got me an autographed picture of the actor Justin Chambers. She also gave me a copy of the keys to her house so I could use the pool whenever I wanted, as it was just a short walk away.

When I lived with my son's mother before my baby was born, she made me feel like a real extension of her life. When she went to the salon, I went to the salon. (For a girl from Minnesota, getting a blowout in a Beverly Hills Salon off Rodeo Drive felt amazing.) When she went to lunch or to a dinner party, I went, too. She sought not only to include me, but to help me build my own life.

For example, I'd wanted to be a sports attorney or pursue a career in sports advertising, and she set me up with lunches and meetings with people from CNN and Turner Broadcasting—all amazing women I could learn from!

I appreciated these connections and opportunities very much, and I still keep in touch with these people. The connections were and are very real—not fake. Still, I used them to help perpetuate the story I had been telling on social media: that I'd moved out to California for an internship. Still, many of my friends and some of my family didn't even know I was pregnant, and I had little communication with anyone back home. The whole time I was in California, my dad only called twice to discuss contracts. Someone in my family even said I was selling my son rather than placing him for adoption. Home was a mess, and my reality was a mess, too—so I distanced myself from them as much as possible.

"Dinner party tonight! Time to network!" I included under another photo, my belly cropped out.

"Almost time for my first LA business lunch!" I wrote on Instagram, showing a photo of my face only.

At one of those lunches, as we sat waiting for her friend to join us, we had an incredible moment: we decided on a name in the most miraculous way. Ever since I'd chosen her as my baby's adoptive mother, I'd given her full autonomy over decisions, within reason. I asked a version of "What do you want? You didn't get to be pregnant," at every opportunity. While waiting for one of her friends from CNN to come talk to me about an internship, I continued that theme—only this time, I asked about a name.

"What do you think you're going to name him?" I asked.

"I have a couple names picked out. There's one I really like, though. I think it sounds powerful."

Then, she told me, and it *did* sound powerful—and amazing for another reason. I couldn't believe it. The name she'd chosen as the baby's middle name was a family name for me. In fact, my dad had always told us that the first-born grandson should have that middle name. It was incredible.

"You've got to be kidding me!" I said. "It's my brother's

middle name, my dad's middle name, and my grandma's last name."

She had no idea! It was just one more example of our connection and how I believe it was all meant to be.

TO MINNESOTA AND BACK AGAIN

In planning for the baby's birth, we toured Cedars-Sinai Medical Center and discussed all our options. Did we want to be in the same room or conjoining rooms? (We opted for the same room, as insurance wouldn't cover the other option.) Did we want a doula? (My son's mother said she'd find me one I clicked with, if I wanted.) For every consideration, we'd sit down and talk about it together. I always deferred to what my son's mother wanted.

It was the plan all along for my son's mother to be in the delivery room when the baby was born. I was allowed one support person with me via the California adoption laws, and I wavered on who would take the spot. For a long time, I'd decided to have my friend Bethany there. Ultimately, though, I decided on my mom, even though she and I had our struggles. Looking back, it was my codependency on her, and also I didn't want to hurt her feelings.

The idea was for the support person to come visit me before and during the birth, but we all decided it would be easier if, instead, we flew back to Minnesota for a week-end. First, we cleared it with my doctor, Jay Goldberg—a phenomenal human being and a wonderful physician. He said I was nearing the point where it wouldn't be safe to fly, so we'd better book the tickets. We did, over the weekend of August 12, I think.

My memories from this trip are a bit spurty. We didn't tell any of my siblings or friends we were coming because we didn't want to make it a thing, so it was just my stepdad, mom, and my little brother, Riley, at the house. My son's mother even brought Riley a gift. As a group, we went boating once—gently, of course—and we also went for a drive. Otherwise, we didn't leave the house. I didn't want to see anyone.

There was some friction between my son's mom and my mom. At the time, part of me thought it was because my mom thought this other woman was taking over the maternal role for me—which, in a way, she was. I don't know exactly what happened, but one morning when I was sleeping in (I've never been an early riser), both the moms in my life had a conversation that would alter their relationship forever.

My mom said that as they sipped their coffee one morn-ing, my son's mother told her a story about a client who overstepped the boundaries of the birthmother/adoptive mother contract. She may have just been telling a story, but what my mom heard was, "Back off. You're telling me to know my place." There was another moment, too, when we were out for a drive: my son's mother called herself my "sugar mama" because she was paying my stipend, and it rubbed my mom the wrong way. She couldn't handle it. She still can't, to this day. Even now, when they communicate, my mom will bring up how hard the adoption has been on me and the family, and I hear about that communication from my son's mother. It was challenging then, and it's challenging now.

Overall, the trip back to Minnesota before I gave birth was something I needed more than anyone. Mostly, I think I needed to see my little brother. When I was there, Riley let me sleep with Ellie, his favorite stuffed animal. He warmed me. I remember longing for my brother—for him to be running around, splashing in the water with me, or being crazy. I wanted him to bother me in that cute, young way. I needed the perfect love only kids can give—pure, unfazed, unconditional. He didn't see me as broken. He loved me with no strings. He didn't treat me like something to be ashamed of, or want something from. I never had to talk about adoption with him, or being a birthmother, or pregnancy, or contracts.

We watched cartoons. He saw me and loved me anyway. That made the trip worth it.

My parents always thought Riley found out about my pregnancy along with the rest of the world—later, when I lived in DC and changed a blog I maintained (*20-something Birthmother*) from anonymous to something that came from me. However, I recently discovered Riley knew well before that—a weekend at the lake, when I couldn't take him on the Jet Ski like I used to.

Smart kid.

A BABY SHOWER AND MIXED EMOTIONS

Just over a month later, we had the baby shower with my son's mother, her family, and her friends at the trendy and famous Chateau Marmont, just like we'd talked about in the car on my first visit to LA

The shower was a beautiful cocktail party in one of the suites. We had two photos propped up on the piano of both she and I as children, and some people could not tell who was who. That's how alike we looked as kids—little blonde, curly-headed girls. The shower was attended by many of her friends and family whom I'd met, and others I hadn't. My main memory of the event was feeling overwhelmed, like it was all superficial in a way yet knowing it wasn't. I knew they cared about me, and they worked to make the shower about me, too. They toasted both of us.

Her friends and family checked in on me several times throughout the night, simply asking if I was okay.

Was I okay? Not really.

Looking around, I felt joy because I saw firsthand how much love my baby would have in his life. Still, part of me was breaking: all this celebrating of someone else gaining a child—but, for that to happen, I had to lose one.

In reality, I knew the night was not about me. I wasn't sad because I had *wanted* it that way—I wanted her to have that moment, and I had never once considered changing my mind. But I also wanted to be celebrated. In my heart, I think I saw that night as the first step to my being forgotten. My son's mother had asked me if I wanted to be at the shower, and I'd agreed. I'd agreed to *all* of it—but there, in that moment, it became too much. I escaped to the bathroom to cry. One of my son's mother's friends walked in and found me.

The party wound down, and we all went back to her house.

Still, my emotions that night reminded me of a time not long before that, when we were on the beach. A man had walked up to me. I must have either looked miserable or like I was glowing, because I was just about ready to pop. In those final days, I remember every moment had a special kind of energy to it.

"My wife always told me never to ask this, but I know that face," he said. "When are you due?"

The short answer? *I'm due in just over a week.* I thought. The long answer? *It's really another woman who is due.*

I dug my toes a little deeper into the sand and felt my son kick in my belly.

CHAPTER FOUR

♥

He's Here!

The morning of my son's birth, I woke up at 6:00 a.m. next to my mom, who'd flown in the day before. We were all at my son's mother's house. We'd done a lot of walking the day before.

"Oh my God, it won't stop!" I yelled. "I just peed myself!"

I'd never had a baby before, obviously, so my first reaction to my water breaking was to think I had a bladder control issue. But my mom knew better.

We woke my son's mother up and began to discuss what we should do next. When we'd toured Cedars-Sinai in West Hollywood, the hospital where I'd give birth, they'd told me not to panic when my water broke. They advised against coming in until I started having contractions; we could call, but there was no need to rush to the hospital.

I wasn't having contractions yet. My mom thought we should leave immediately, but my son's mother thought we should wait longer based on what the hospital had said. I agreed.

Really, though, I didn't give a shit who was right or wrong; I knew what I was supposed to do, and I just wanted to take a shower.

My mom said I could get bacteria from showering, but my son's mother said she thought it would be fine.

From those early moments, the division of the day reared its head—and it was about to get worse. It set the tone for what was to come of the day and even my larger experience: I didn't feel like I was in control. Not even that, but it was almost like I felt silenced. I knew all the hard decisions had been made, but still I wanted some of the little ones to go my way. I felt gross because my water had just broken, and for some reason I wanted to shave my legs because the doctor was about to be all up in there. (It turns out shaving your legs at nine months pregnant is exactly as hard as it sounds.)

So I did. I got up and walked to the bathroom. As I stood

under the running water, my thoughts raced. *What the hell?* I thought. *This day is supposed to be about me, and I already don't have a voice.*

While I was in the shower, my son's mother was making arrangements to reschedule her patients for the day. My mom, who is a painter, had gone out on the front steps to paint, presumably to calm herself down.

We had a birthing plan: both support people—the two moms in my life—would be in the room. My son's mother would cut the umbilical cord. Every detail and special touch—from the music that would be played in the room to my first meal after giving birth—had been discussed well in advance so we'd be ready by the time we actually headed to the hospital.

At least, that was the plan.

THE CHEROKEE QUESTION

Sitting in the intake area of the hospital, I received a text from my son's father—out of the blue. There's no way he would have known I was in labor; it was the craziest thing. I didn't respond because I had other things to deal with: namely, the two strong women with me.

There's a question that comes up inevitably on every

adoption form: whether or not either birth parent has any Cherokee as part of their ancestry. To my knowledge, if Cherokee linage is present, the tribe can have rights over the baby. When the question was presented to us at intake at Cedars, my mom—out of the blue—began to wonder aloud whether or not we had any Cherokee in our family.

I'd heard talk that we may have some Native American ancestry, but it was just that: talk. Lots of people think that where I'm from. My mom wasn't even certain by any stretch of the imagination, and here she was bringing it up literally hours before I was about to have a baby. (Note: I recently had a 23andMe test done, and it was confirmed that I don't have even 1 percent of Native American in me. One hundred percent European.)

Thinking the whole adoption could be reversed, I started crying and freaking out. My son's mother was understandably worked up, too. We were scared. She got on the phone with the attorneys while my mom got on the phone to ask my grandma if she knew whether we had any Cherokee in us. My grandmother, of course, didn't know either.

Eventually, the lawyers examined the family register, and they found I did not, in fact, have any Cherokee in me. Crisis averted—except it really wasn't because the whole time, I was in labor, trying to console my son's mother and making sure she still wanted to go through with it. I believe she thought my mom had done it on purpose, and my mom thought she was just asking a question—I think. To this day, I don't know what is true. All I know is that these were the last hours I'd have my baby inside me, close to me, and I wanted to spend them peacefully. The whole event was a tragedy on an already tragic day. I missed him already.

HAPPY BIRTHDAY, MY BOY

Shortly after the Cherokee fiasco, I was moved to the birthing suite—a truly beautiful space overlooking the LA hills and the famous Hollywood sign. It felt like a movie. I was three centimeters dilated. A long way to go.

I hadn't had any contractions yet, so my first memory of the room—other than it being beautiful and the staff being so kind—was of hunger. I was starving, but I wasn't allowed to eat after intake. *How do they expect you to push a human out of your body when you're depleted?* I wondered. Someone—I can't remember who—went out and got food, and my son's mom snuck me a small piece of chocolate. The day shift nurse seemed to sense the tension in the room, giving me extra attention and being sweet. I was genuinely sad when the shifts changed and she had to go.

Although it had been hours, I still hadn't had any contractions. As I sat on the yoga ball in the room, I realized I had to go number two. After returning from the bathroom, my son's mother suggested we go for a walk down the hall to push things along. Suddenly, walking back to the room after one loop around the wing, I felt the worst pain in the world. It debilitated me. I could barely walk.

Good God—the things women's bodies can do.

When I got back to the room, they checked me again: almost there. Quite the development. Maybe I was having smaller contractions before that I'd just never felt, but I definitely felt that one. And the two after that.

Cedars had an anesthesiologist on the birthing floor, so I didn't need to wait long for my epidural. Dr. Goldberg came in shortly after that, and we made a plan.

"You could start pushing now, but I think that'd be a long birth," he said. "I think you're ready, but we should labor you down so your body has more time to relax and open up."

We agreed waiting was best.

"Are you sure?" he said, smiling. "I've got a meeting coming up that I really don't want to go to. I'd love to get out of it."

It was a bit of comic relief, and I needed it.

He was gone a short amount of time, and I took a nap. (Those epidurals, man. Wonderful.) While I rested, my mom held the heart monitor over my belly, making sure it was in the right spot. She also rubbed my back and my feet, doing all these tiny beautiful things that got lost in the flurry of the birth and the turmoil that came after. (These are details I'd forgotten until I started writing this book, and they're extra special to me today.)

Dr. Goldberg came back in and checked me immediately.

"We're good to go," he said, and the room transformed into a flurry of activity. I was very scared that I was going to poop, although the nurses had assured me all day long that it would be no big deal if I did.

I even shaved my legs for this, I thought. *Please don't let me shit myself.*

Each mom in my life held one of my legs, while my baby's soon-to-be grandmother videotaped. I don't know if my body knew—or, I like to think now—that my son knew that I couldn't handle any more stress that day.

Push, rest.

Push, rest.

Push, rest.

An intense pressure. I wasn't even supposed to push, but the pressure was so intense that I couldn't *not* push.

Then, he was here. My beautiful baby boy. The doctor said the umbilical cord was the longest he'd ever seen—something he said contributes to intelligence. If he was telling the truth or trying to lighten the mood in the room, I'll never know.

As we'd discussed beforehand, he came out and went straight to his adoptive mother's chest—a moment I'd replay over and over in the years to come, wondering if he was scared and confused. This haunted me for a long time and still does to this day. I know how important it is that they created that bond, but was it traumatizing for him to not come to my chest? Was he scared to come out of me and go to another person? That keeps me up at night.

In that moment, I wanted to hold him. At the time, though, I didn't know how to advocate for myself, didn't know it was okay to say I wanted time. In that moment, too, I was still in the post-delivery phase. The pressure of delivering the placenta—which, for some reason, was almost worse than the pain of delivering the baby—was top of mind. That and my grief.

I was sobbing uncontrollably. I looked at my son, then looked away. At him, then away. I was almost physically holding my face so I wouldn't stare.

I had a ton of emotions: I was happy he was okay, but I was also deeply sad. My focus was trying to keep it together. *I've got all these people in here who will start to freak out if I start to cry or show too much emotion, so I'm not allowed to*, I thought. *I'm not allowed to have that moment and say I need to hold him, to smell him, to feel him, to be with him for a little while.* I simply never felt like I was safe to have those experiences, and that's not anything anyone necessarily did or didn't do; it's just the way I felt. Looking back, I wonder why I didn't use my voice.

All along, I'd known I was going to have a hard time, but I never once thought about changing my mind. I knew I had to do this for my son, and I was safe and secure in my choice. But there was a feeling in the room that changed the temperature: people were so worried I was going to change my mind that I didn't feel like I could step on their toes by asking for what I needed. I didn't use my voice, and I felt powerless—like a vessel whose job was done. Like I wanted to disappear, or maybe like I already had. Ultimately, I'd taken myself and my needs out of the equation because I thought that was best for my son. I'd have given anything to hold him close to my chest then. I still would.

There was so much tragedy in that room, and there was so much beauty.

THE MELTDOWN

After my son was born, we were moved out of the birthing suite and into a different room. Many of the special touches we'd discussed—my post-birth meal included—fell by the wayside. I know it sounds like a little detail, but it was big to me. Although I know nobody meant for it to be that way, I couldn't help but feel like I was already forgotten. Like I'd done my job.

That night, my son's mother and I slept, and our moms took turns holding the baby—he never went to the nursery, because that's how my son's mother wanted it.

When I woke up that morning, it was time: check-out day. It had all happened so fast. I remember bits and pieces. I was in pain, physically and emotionally. A social worker walked in—one from the hospital, not the one we had been working with. She was by-the-book, ensuring I'd been treated right by Cedars and that I wasn't coerced into the adoption situation. I wasn't, of course, and I was secure in my decision. I told her as much and answered all her questions about how wonderful the hospital staff had been. Was it emotional? Yes. Did I have any doubts? No.

The room emptied as both moms in my life went out into the hallway so I could have my conversation. While they were in the hall together, it happened. What happened, exactly, I'll never know—but I've heard it secondhand from both sides. I don't know who is telling the truth, but I think it's possible they both are. They're speaking to their experience, after all. My mom said things needed to slow down and that I needed time. My son's mother freaked out, understandably. Then, commotion. Screaming. I was still stuck in the room, trying to get the social worker to hurry. I didn't know what was going on, but I knew it wasn't good.

The social worker left, and my mom came into the room. She was screaming. I had no idea where my son's mom and grandma went. In that moment, all I knew was that there was trouble.

"What did you do?" I screamed at my mom, repeating it over and over. "What did you fucking do?"

It was chaos. My mom started grabbing her things frantically and stuffing them into her bag, saying she was leaving and that this was crazy.

The situation escalated. I stood up and walked to the bathroom. There were so many fluids—the tears, the blood from my IV that ripped out when I stood up, the blood gushing from my body.

A mere twelve hours before, I'd given birth. Now, I was being discharged soon, my mom was losing it, and my son's mother was gone. I sobbed, leaning against the cold tile wall. When I came out of the bathroom some time later—it's all a blur—I finally got to hold my son, *alone*. For the first time. My mom was gone to who-knows-where. I had a few quiet moments with him before another social worker walked in. I was told it was the social worker who was going to try to help me work things out with my mom. I had a good relationship with that social worker. Once, while at my son's mother's house discussing details with her, Sadie ate my burrito. It was always a running joke between the three of us that the dog owed me a burrito!

This time, she wanted to talk paperwork—specifically, a document that shrinks the amount of time a birthmother has to change her mind from thirty days to forty-eight hours. I'd agreed to sign the document a month before when the social worker came to the house and explained the post-delivery paperwork; I simply didn't want my son's mother to live that month in fear. I wondered if she'd be able to love him fully until that grace period was over.

My arms were a contradiction: with my left, I held my beautiful newborn baby; with my right, I signed the papers to expedite making him someone else's son, too.

ON MY OWN

Later, I'd learn that checking birthmothers out of the hospital as soon as possible after giving birth is what is recommended to adoptive parents, though I didn't know it at the time. Later, I'd also learn that while I was signing papers, alone with my son, my son's mother had taken my mom back to her house to gather our clothes and possessions and driven her to check into the hotel. It had always been our plan to stay in a hotel that night—looking back, though, I'm not sure why we'd opted for that. My mom was going to help care for me at the hotel; I'd just had a baby, after all—a baby who would be home with *his* mother.

A short time later, I checked out of the hospital, and my son's mother came to pick me up. She dropped me off at the hotel she'd also taken my mom to, but there was only one problem: I couldn't find my mom. The plan was for me to stay there for a couple of days to recover—my mom at my side—but she was nowhere to be found. She was my support person, and she was gone.

I stood alone in my room, losing it. My body hurt. I still

looked pregnant. I needed to sit down because standing was too painful, but I didn't know what to do with myself once I sat down. I managed to walk across the road to the gas station and buy two packs of cigarettes—which I chain-smoked as I sat on the balcony, sobbing. I hadn't told anyone what had happened yet—not my son's father, nobody. I just wanted my mom. I tried calling her cell over and over. I tried the front desk to see if they'd connect me to her room. Nobody would tell me how to reach her or where she was. I got ahold of my stepdad, who said, "You guys need to stay away from each other."

Stay away from each other? She came out to help me. *I just gave birth,* I thought. *What the fuck am I supposed to do?* I wondered. I was twenty-one years old. I didn't know the first thing about post-natal care. Am I allowed to shower? When do I take my medicine? Normally, the nurses would have been taking care of me at this time, but I had checked out early. I didn't have anybody there with me. In the moment, I felt so alone.

During my time in the hotel, I received a Facebook message from my dad. "How are you doing?" it read. I replied and told him my son was born. Then, he said, "If I wouldn't have messaged you, would you even have told me?"

I didn't know the answer to that.

Eventually, I was so desperate that I Facetimed my sister, Amber, and asked if she'd stay on the line with me while I was in the shower. I was bleeding and didn't know if it was too much. She had been trying to get ahold of my mom, too, to have her come and check on me. All Amber wanted was someone there to hold me, to check my bleeding, to cuddle me—to do everything you are meant to do for a woman after she gives birth.

I was glad my sister was on the line because I didn't want to pass out or fall and nobody know. That night I slept alone, wrapped in hotel blankets. Still bleeding.

The next night, I finally got my mom's room number from the front desk. I put on a pair of slippers, plodded my way to her door, and began to noise-complaint-level bang on it. She opened it, then shut it in my face. When she finally opened it, she began to tell me how she didn't feel good. (Spoiler alert: I didn't either. I just had a baby.) How my son's mother and I "deserved each other." Saying I shouldn't be in her room.

My mom said when the social worker came into the hospital room the day before, I gave her a "look" that made everybody think I was changing my mind—which I never was. I was having a moment, a feeling—which I was fucking entitled to—that got blown up. My mom then tried to advocate for me by telling my son's mother I needed more time, and it escalated into the fight in the hallway. In her memory, she was issued a no-contact, meaning she wasn't permitted to contact me within forty-eight hours of the events of the hospital—something I'd never initiated or signed off on.

I was livid. I checked out of the hotel and took my bags to my son's mother's house, the place I'd been living, and planned to stay for a couple of days. My memories here are a blur, but I remember sitting on her couch, wearing a green tank top and feeding my son. Then, I recall saying how much I needed *my own* mother. Even though I felt like she'd abandoned me. Even though she ignored over one hundred of my calls hours after I'd given birth. I needed my mom; we've always had that type of relationship. She could scream at me, hold me in a doorway, yell at me, lock me out—and I could do the same to her—and half an hour later, I'd just want her to love me. From that couch, I called my mom and asked if I could come back. She said yes. We walked to the Chinese place that night, at her suggestion, and ordered way too much food. Walking hurt, but I did it anyway.

While there, I got a text from my son's father, asking how I was doing. My son's mother had let him know the baby had arrived. I told him the baby was beautiful. I slept in my mom's room that night.

The day we were set to leave LA, we went to Hugo's—my favorite breakfast place—and then to the house to say goodbye. I vividly remember seeing a yellow butterfly on the way there; it was like time stopped. I felt like I could see its individual wing flaps in slow motion, like it was telling me something, like it was an example of time slowing down. I could see the individual pattern on its wings, which I learned symbolize hope, guidance, and peace. It was like my mind was giving me a sign of what I needed to see.

It was the first time the moms in my life had been in the same room since the blowup, and I was worried. Because we were saying goodbye, though, everyone was respectful, and my mom and I both got to hold my son. They gave me a moment with him, alone. Inside my head, I was panicking. *I can't leave him*, I thought. *I don't know what to do*. I knew he should be with his mother, but I wanted to be closer than states away. *I can't leave him. I don't know what to do. I need more time. I know he's hers now, but I need more time*. My head played these thoughts on loop.

"This is not your fault," I whispered into his sweet-smelling head. "Don't be angry at me. I will always be here for you. I will always love you."

CHAPTER FIVE

♥

Trying to Rebuild

As I walked into the airport to leave California—and a part of myself—behind, I struggled, both physically and emotionally. My mom and I had another shouting match in the car on the way there, and we weren't speaking. We'd stopped off at the lawyer's office, where I asked for a copy of my son's birth certificate with my name on it and received a check for the final two months of expenses his mother had agreed to cover. The check exchange added another argument with my mom; you could have cut the tension in that office with a knife. In the parking garage, I had to apologize to the Uber driver for all the screaming on the way to the airport. That poor man.

I felt like we were leaving earlier than I'd wanted for one reason: because I needed to get her out of there. She couldn't keep her cool. I was rushed and angry. It could have been a defense mechanism, in retrospect, and I could have been blaming her for feelings I couldn't yet identify for myself. Still, I was pissed. She kept saying she didn't feel good—and neither did I, considering I'd just had a baby two and a half days earlier and was carrying all my luggage alone. Every step hurt. My heart hurt, too. I kept putting my hands on my stomach, holding it tenderly. I was bawling all over the place, not just because of the fight with my mom and the fact that she wasn't helping me like I wanted her to, but also because I was leaving. I knew I wanted to go home—but what home? Not my son's mother's home. Not my mom's home. Not my sister's home. Did I have a home? I had no idea. On top of the physical and emotional pain, I felt lost.

When we landed in Minnesota, my mom said she was too tired to drive the two hours home.

You're too tired? I thought. But I got in the driver's seat anyway.

We got pulled over on the way home, too, because I was speeding. My mom told the cop my sister had just placed a child for adoption, as if hoping for a reprieve—a fact that wasn't even true, obviously. After a little back and forth, he let us go with a warning.

A HOME, UNRAVELING

I stayed at my mom and stepdad's house for about two weeks after I returned to Minnesota, and the only way I can describe that time was that it was an utter shit show. I missed my son horribly. As I wrote on my blog at the time, "I know that my son is living a life I could never give him now, but I can't help but be so mad at myself. Why did I do it? Why did I think I wasn't enough?"

I explained more in another post, dated around that time:

> Some people may know from the beginning how real it is, but I did not. Of course I could feel him inside me and I could see him move in my belly and grow, but I never felt how I do now, until he came out and I saw what I had created. He was real. This was a real person. A person that would grow up and do such extraordinary things. I am already so proud of him. He truly is the best thing I EVER did and always will be. He will always be the most important part of my life and the most important part of me. Every day, my first thought will be him and every night my last thought will be him.

During this emotional struggle (to put it mildly), I was still trying to get my college coursework done online, as I'd been doing throughout my entire pregnancy (even taking an exam from the hospital while I was in labor). Most of my professors didn't even know I was pregnant because

I'd lied, telling them I had family emergencies. The one professor I did tell was kind and had helped me get a scholarship the year before. It was hard to keep my focus, however, with everything going on at home.

My mom and I continued to be at war with one another, screaming at the top of our lungs daily. This wasn't normal arguing. My mom called me names, at one point even saying my adoption was fraudulent. I remember sitting in my car, not sure what to do—calling the lawyers, calling my son's mother. I can't even recall the specific order of events when I look back, which speaks to the blur of it all. I was so emotional, having just given birth, so I often responded to my mother with names of my own. *She was the one who supported my decision and even told me I wouldn't be a good mom,* I thought. *Why is she so angry with me?*

My hormones were going haywire during this time, too. That first week, my milk dropped. I didn't know what to do with myself. Should I be pumping the milk and sending it to my baby? Did he need it? When I asked his mother, she said I was a twenty-one-year-old woman who should be out living my life, not worrying about pumping milk every day. She was right, but on some level, I just wanted to help. I wanted to be close to him.

The whole experience was traumatic. I was literally missing my son, leaking, not sure what to do. I remember going to grab a cocktail with a couple of friends—just a catch-up drink, nothing crazy. When I woke up the next morning, my bed was soaked with milk and tears.

After I'd been home for about a week, my mom and step-dad took a scheduled vacation to Utah. They needed someone to take care of my little brother—and, of course, I was there. I'd long ago asked my family to keep the birth a secret, and they did. I was ashamed and felt like people would judge me, still feeling like *birthmother* was a dirty word. So, when I watched my little brother, he still didn't know anything that had happened. It was difficult to play mom to my younger brother, having just placed my own baby for adoption. At the same time, it was wonderful because he brought me so much comfort, as he always has. I made him fruit and spinach smoothies every morn-ing—along with French toast—just like my son's mother had taught me when I lived with her in LA I was recreat-ing the good times.

When my mom and stepdad returned, the fighting between my mom and I re-escalated. Once, when I was trying to leave the situation, she held me in the door, blood and fluids still seeping out of me. I found out she'd been calling the attorneys and saying God-knows-what to them—and, obviously, they billed by the hour. Then, I'd call them back and try to figure out what was going on.

Our arguments were not healthy. She hadn't had time to grieve what had happened, and neither had I. We just took it out on each other; our house was a battlefield. My mom was so angry with my son's mother that she wanted her to cover expenses like gas to and from the airport and increases to our insurance premium—which, I later discovered, was a non-issue, as I was double-covered from the beginning. It never went to my step-dad and mom's insurance; my dad's insurance covered the entire bill.

It wasn't just my mom. I still hadn't made up with my sister or my older brother. I didn't feel like I had anyone to talk to, even though my sister and stepdad both reached out to me. Even my dad, who I'd become closer to, reached out again and offered me a place to stay. I was too closed off. I did feel like I maybe had a couple friends to lean on, but those friends were living regular college-kid lives. I, on the other hand, was living in a post-partum war zone. I had so many emotions and no idea what to do with them. I didn't feel like I could text or call my son's mother, which is really what I wanted to do. I knew she was caring for a newborn, and it had been tossed around so many times—by my mom and by the attorneys—that she would be done with me after my son was placed. I heard it enough times that I began to believe it.

I had nowhere to go that felt safe. I felt like a walking burden to everyone, not even welcomed in a place I once called my home. My whole excuse for not leaving—to somewhere, anywhere—was that I was waiting on the remainder of my belongings to come from my son's mother's house, where I'd been living. Maybe it was a defense mechanism; maybe I was hoping my mom would have been who I needed her to be then. Looking back, I wish I would have just left; I deserved to be treated better than that, even if I was lashing out, too. Although I was now a parent myself, I was not the parent in that situation. I may have been suffering from post-pregnancy brain, but I still didn't have the maturity of my mom, speaking simply in years.

At around the two-week mark, I asked my stepdad out to lunch at our go-to place: McDonald's. He used to take me there on the first day of school, as a ritual. It was our special spot.

"What should I do?" I asked him. We talked about how things weren't good at home.

"You need to leave," he said, on the verge of tears. I could tell it hurt him to say.

"What?" I asked.

"Listen, I'm looking out for both of you," he said. "You guys can't do this anymore. It's no longer doable." He was coming from a place of love, looking out for me, my mom, my little brother, and himself, too.

He was right. The events of those weeks—and the circumstances and all that had happened before them—ruined my relationship with my mother for a long time. My belongings arrived that next day, with a cute little heart note from my son's mother on top of the box, just like I'd had a feeling she'd leave. I immediately packed them into my car and drove to Iowa to move in with my sister Amber—the one who had driven me to the abortion clinic, the one who was now pregnant herself after trying seemingly forever, and the one who had always been in my corner. I had an internship lined up with her company and was hopeful the move would be a fresh start.

It wasn't, really.

FROM ANGER TO DEPRESSION

My sister was kind, as always, and gave me the opportunity to do an internship at her company, and I was grateful. Without that, I would have likely had to take a semester off. Because the internship was unpaid, though, I knew I needed to get an additional job to pay my bills. I got hired at a restaurant—a Buffalo Wild Wings—as a server a few nights a week. With my sister and brother-in-law both working during the day, sometimes I skipped the internship altogether because I couldn't get out of bed. I was so fucking sad that I couldn't move my body. I remember her dog and cat lying on me, none of us moving.

As a server, there were weeks I'd work four nights in a row and then have three nights off—which, again, led to me spending more time alone in my bed, sobbing. The days I didn't work were miserable. The days I did work were okay; the interaction started to help, and I made connections with my coworkers that helped breathe a little life back into me. One of my coworkers at Buffalo Wild Wings got pregnant when I worked there, and she was talking about what she was going to do. It was crazy; pregnancy seemed to follow me.

Then, the drinking started picking back up again. That was just what we did for fun; we'd get off at the end of a shift and go out. It is part of the culture of the service industry, in my experience.

My life started to spiral then, but slowly at first. I met a guy who was bad news. I knew he wasn't a truthful person, but I didn't care. The calls from my son's mother had stopped coming as frequently, and I thought what everyone said was coming true: she was forgetting about me. And if she was, then so was my baby.

I became obsessed with anything distracting—drinking

and using Tinder. I was hyper-sexual. I'd been like that before I had my son, but my issues heightened significantly after I had him.

Not all my choices were sexual, though. I even transformed myself in other ways. For example, my son's mother drove a Prius, and I leased one, too—not because I was crazy or a stalker, but because subconsciously, I was trying to re-create my life in California. I went to yoga every other day, drank green smoothies, and tried to go vegan—all while getting blackout drunk with my work friends after our shifts.

The truth is that after my baby was born, I had to mourn losing his adoptive mother, too. That was so hard. She had become like a mother to me, and I felt doubly traumatized. Sometimes, I felt a sense of panic around the loss. I remember one day, I was on a walk and I just needed my son. I'd been having a semi-panic attack all day. I called my son's mother and asked if I could fly out to see him because I just needed to hold him. She said to give it time, as everyone was still adjusting. I don't remember if I dreamed this or not, but I feel like I remember her saying, "You don't want him back, right?" She was as scared as I was, sometimes, I think.

I was also sad to leave California, which took me years of therapy to be able to admit. I'm from the Midwest, and the people there aren't bad by any means. But the people on the West Coast were different than any I'd ever encountered: they were accepting, and I was allowed to have feelings. I didn't feel like a burden there. I didn't feel judged. And I lost all that, too, when I lost my son.

I had ups and downs while living with Amber, but none of the downs were her fault. It was difficult living with her because she was pregnant and I'd just given birth, but I couldn't have imagined being anywhere else—besides, of course, LA. Amber has been and always will be my person. Being with her gave me room to breathe. She's always supported me, holding me while I've cried on more occasions than I can recall. I remember laying on her couch, watching *Law and Order SVU*, during some dark moments of my depression when even moving felt hard. Looking back, I know I should have worked a lot harder at the internship she was kind enough to get me, but I just wasn't capable then—and she knew it. She let me be who I needed to be in those moments, and I'm forever grateful to her for that.

She had wonderful neighbors—Irish sisters—who would cheer me up when I was down. I'd go sit with them in their garage when I wasn't working, and we'd talk for hours. They helped pull me out of some of my down moments, as did many of my friends at Buffalo Wild Wings and my brother-in-law. Mostly, though, when I thought about my son, I cried by myself. I pushed my feelings down and tried to ignore them, hoping they'd go away.

After a few months of living with my sister, I returned to Saint Paul to resume classes. The first time I was in school in Saint Paul, I lived in a house with roommates. I'd found the place on Craigslist—a necessity, as it was second semester, and everyone had already found housing by that point. I remember Skyping the owner and agreeing to the lease without ever seeing the house or meeting the occupants first. I partied all the time; I'd come home shit-faced and leave the door open, was loud in my room at all hours of the night, and had random men over—typical college shenanigans, at least of those in my crowd. I wasn't making the best decisions, but I wasn't crazy, either—at least, that was the justification I made to myself. Instead of comparing myself to college students who were doing far better than me as the norm, I compared myself to those in a circle I had intentionally selected. It was a tool I'd later learn I used to normalize my behavior—and it wasn't the first time. I'd repeat the cycle later, in California, when I hung with two different groups of people.

When I moved back to college the second time after living with my sister, I lived alone. The drinking was no longer a social event—it was just what I needed. I drowned myself in alcohol—absolutely drowned myself. I was waitressing, this time at a restaurant called Old Chicago, and I also lobbied at the state capitol as part of my courses. I'd even get recognized by customers who'd seen me on the news from my lobbying work. I vividly remember standing on the steps, getting ready to fight for a bill to combat drunk driving, hungover as hell. I also vividly remember being interviewed on the radio, knowing I was still drunk from the night before and praying nobody would notice.

I want to be clear: I did a lot of good in this time, too. I worked very hard, spending sometimes forty-hour weeks at the capitol lobbying for bills I did care about, all the while taking a large course load. This outward success allowed me to hide my inner turmoil. As I wrote on my blog at the time,

> I don't want to be scared. I want to be strong. I want to be the person everyone in my life is expecting me to be. How do I tell them I am not that person anymore? I am not the strong woman who they once knew. The people who know about my son expect me to be this strong and ambitious woman. The people who don't know about my son expect the same, too. They constantly are asking, "What's wrong with you," or saying, "You seem so different." Or, the most common, "Where have you been? I never see you," because of the massive amount of alone time and hiding I do. All I want to do is take time to grieve. I can't do that. I don't get to do that. I am expected to jump back up on my

feet and keep going. When will I ever process all of this, or when will I ever let myself process all of this? When will I stop letting my fear get in the way of my happiness? What's it going to take for that to happen?

There were times I wanted to kill myself. I looked fine on the outside, but on the inside, I didn't know what the fuck to do. I spent so much energy trying to be the person I thought my son deserved: a birthmother who made the right decision for him, but who was now going to go conquer the world and make him proud. I put so much pressure on myself to meet that goal, including being invited to professional events for my school. Still, many of the things I did were in opposition to that goal. It was never good enough. I'd work so hard during the day—excelling in school, appearing to have it all together—that I'd come home emotionally fucked and drained. Then, I'd go out and drink all night, black out, and not know how I got home—or, sometimes, who was there with me. I felt like I needed it, though, to talk about my baby. I never talked about him to anyone at college during the day, and most of my friends didn't even know I'd had a baby.

I remember when I told one of my close friends about my son. It was my first time flying back to see him in LA for my birthday. I needed a ride to the airport, and on the way, I told my friend, "I'm going to see my son." She was in shock. I showed her pictures on my phone. It was the first time I told her—and one of the few times I'd told anyone I knew, up to that point.

When I was out at bars, though, and met strangers—I talked about him all the time. It was therapeutic. They were supportive. They lifted me up. Still, to say it wasn't healthy would be the understatement of the century.

It all came to a head the night I lost a special necklace.

Before I left California, my son's mother gave me a necklace with three lightning bolts—one for me, one for her, and one for our son. She had a matching one. One night, I went out with my friends to a Mardi Gras-style party. I don't remember much besides the Bacardi rum. To this day, I don't remember where I was, who I was with, or who brought me home. When I woke up, all my necklaces were gone. My shoes were strewn about the bottom level. I couldn't find my coat. My sweater was in a corner upstairs.

I broke down and called both my son's mother and my mom. Out loud, I told them both that I needed help to curb my drinking. In my head, it was a different story. It was more dire: *I'm going to fucking die. I'm going to drink myself to death, get into an accident, or get murdered. I can't control myself. If my whole life is going to be spent not being able to pick myself up off some bathroom floor, what good is it?*

They both supported me and encouraged me to go to counseling, so I started seeing my school counselor at Concordia. It helped a little, but I stopped going when I hit a plateau in my progress. In reality, the most helpful part of that experience was saying out loud that I needed support. It was something I wasn't used to doing. I think that's because I just wanted somebody to show me I mattered enough and that they'd be there for me. I remember thinking, *Why isn't my mom here?* on several occasions. I'd usually call her when I was messed up, telling her about my problems. She never visited, but I still think a piece of me wanted her to come save me.

GRADUATION

Graduating college was huge for me, for many reasons. A couple of weeks before the big day, my son's mom had slowed down talking to me. I thought something was wrong. Then, in the middle of class, I got a call from her: she said she hadn't wanted to ruin the surprise, but she was gifting me a trip to Hawaii for my graduation present. I was so grateful! I'd invited her to the event itself, as she told me we'd always be part of each other's families. She couldn't come, though, which caused my mind to spin: What about my wedding? What about other big events? What else would my son miss?

The day of graduation itself was very emotional for me.

My mom was doing my hair in the kitchen, and I remember having to go upstairs to cry. I just needed a moment. Walking across the stage later, I felt proud of myself—working my ass off, paying my own way. I wondered if I should be happy or sad. After all, I thought, this was the moment—this was the "why" in terms of why I placed my son for adoption. So both of us could have a better life. I was torn. *All of that pain—for this?* I thought. As I wrote on my blog, "Is this just the beginning of heart-broken big days?"

During that time, I'd been struggling emotionally still, even seeing a guy with the same name as my son. I can't explain why—I just remember I loved saying his name.

Two weeks later, I left for Hawaii. On my layover, I remember wondering what to do with the money my son's mother had gifted me. They'd covered the rental car, and her dad had a house there they'd been gracious enough to let me stay at. As for myself, I had twenty dollars in my pocket. I sat in the airport, doing the math. I ended up going on four Tinder dates while there and trying to make food last. The trip itself was beautiful; I was there for a week, going cliff jumping, scuba diving, and meeting amazing people. I also read on the beach—a book my son's mother got me, and one that I love very much, even today: *Succulent Wild Woman* by Sark. It was uplifting and empowering. I remember thinking, *I need to tell myself these things over and over even after I leave here.* It would be some time before I actually did, though.

ANOTHER MOVE

After I graduated college and got back from Hawaii, I started a job right away. The position involved door-to-door sales. Learning how to talk to people every day was a fantastic experience for me, and it taught me many skills that have propelled me to where I am now in my career. Although it wasn't the best fit and I eventually left that job, I'm grateful for it. Besides the career opportunities it afforded, it also helped my mood to be out in the real world. Every day, I had to trick myself and act like I was having a great day in order to make a sale.

When I left that position, I wasn't sure what to do. I felt antsy. I was able to break my lease without penalty and thought, *Screw it. I'm going to move to Scottsdale, Arizona.*

Why Scottsdale? I had no idea. I just picked it. I started reaching out to connections on LinkedIn who were in the area, asking for suggestions and trying to network.

Then, I Snapchatted a photo of me moving some of my belongings into storage, and an old high school friend, Emily, messaged me.

"If you move to Washington, DC," she said. "I'll come with you! Let's do this together."

Done deal.

Within a couple of weeks of quitting the door-to-door sales job, I'd put my stuff in a storage unit, gotten out of my lease, and found myself driving not to Scottsdale, but east to DC. We planned to stay with Amber's aunt (she and I have different dads), a beautiful woman I called Aunt Becky.

Aunt Becky let us crash at her house for initially what was supposed to be for a couple of days while Emily and I figured out our living situation. Aunt Becky was out of town that particular weekend, but she left us the door code. It was a beautiful gesture—she'd met me maybe three times before that I remember, but she opened up her doors, telling us to make ourselves at home. It speaks to her character.

We ended up staying longer than a weekend. Emily eventually got a job and moved closer to the DC metropolitan area, but I stayed with Aunt Becky for about five months.

Aunt Becky was always so kind to my sister, and she treated me the same way. She had a no-bullshit rule, and she was exceptionally strong. She came from nothing and worked her way up to being the executive of a company—very positive, uplifting, and successful. This was a woman who I needed to be around and who quickly became my biggest role model. God, she was so good to me. She taught me I was worthy, that I was a badass woman, that it was a damn good thing to love yourself. I'd never believed these things before—and, even if I still didn't believe them about myself during those hard months, I at least had the dialog to put to them.

While living in DC, I dated another man who wasn't good for me; he was simply filling a void. I could feel it, thinking, *If I can just get over being depressed, this is done. That way, I can move on.* I went so far as to tell him—and others—I'd had my tubes tied, although I took a pregnancy test twice a week for two years because I was so paranoid.

I had gotten another serving job when I moved to DC, but Aunt Becky was constantly pushing me to use my degree. She wasn't wrong. Still, I wanted to continue to live in that pattern—the party mode, the blacking out. Throughout it all, Aunt Becky both loved me and pushed me to be better.

During that time, I found another sales job at memory-Blue—this time with a business development component. Rather than going door-to-door, I was working for software companies and other major enterprises. I truly loved the job, and it got my foot in the door for where I am today in my career—and my next big adventure: going back to the West Coast. My first day on the job, I'd heard they were opening an office in California.

This was my chance to get back to my son!

"I want in on that," I told my boss.

"Hold on. You just started like five minutes ago," he said. "Let's see how things go."

Things went well because I busted my ass for that company, smashing sales out of the park. When I finally stepped up to the plate, it was a defining moment for me. I started getting out of bed every day. I'd gone to live with my boyfriend at the time—which, in retrospect, was a horrible decision—and my new drive made it more apparent that he wasn't a good fit. He didn't last much longer, but that was a positive because I had a new focus: I wanted to do a good job for my company and in a job I truly loved, yes, but I ultimately wanted to get back to my son.

I'd been in DC for less than a year, and I started packing again, even though I remember my son's mother telling me that our visitation situation wouldn't change if I lived closer (something that foreshadowed my whole life). Still, I was excited and hopeful. I'd been through so much—

even a cancer scare that caused me to have to get my first mammogram at twenty-four. I was ready for a clean slate: I called my good friend Bethany and convinced her to join me on the coast.

We hit the road to what I felt like was a new beginning. Throughout the time I'd been away—in Minnesota, Iowa, and DC—I'd needed my son. I'd called his mom and asked to schedule visits. If it was within the three times per year that was allowed by the agreement, she let me. When I visited, she suggested I stay in a hotel or Airbnb rather than with her because—as she said—she didn't have the room. I would've slept on the couch—but, like always—I just accepted it and didn't argue. The first time I saw my baby on a visit, we played and did bath time. I wrote a blog post about the experience, including this passage:

> I spent that first night watching and helping with his nightly routine. Feeding, baths, massage, dressing, and then sleep. I watched in awe as he so peacefully went through these motions. I watched in awe, as he so perfectly, simply, existed. I watched in awe as he stared at his mom with every move she made. He watched her, observed her, and I knew in those moments that she has given him so much love and care. I knew I would never need to worry about his well-being and love. If I had ever had a doubt (although I didn't), it would have been gone in that moment. I found myself wishing that he would look at me that way. I hoped

that I could make him see me as someone who would always love him and always be there. I wanted to make him laugh like she did, and I knew that by the end of my short visit, I would.

I was so happy but also dying a little bit inside. I went back to my hotel room and sat on the floor of the shower, too weak to stand. I cried until the water turned cold. It was something I'd grow accustomed to over the years: make accommodations away from the house, visit my son, then go back to my empty room and feel so alone.

On that particular visit, when I'd gone back the next day, I went to play with my baby in his room. I was making funny noises and touching his tummy, and he laughed so hard. I thought I could hear his adoptive grandma say in the kitchen, "I've never heard him laugh like that before!" It was a moment that reassured me of our bond and also made it even harder to leave. We had little moments like that each visit then and each visit since; we continue to grow closer.

When I went back for his first birthday, I had the opportunity to spend three full days with him. It was magical. As I wrote on my blog, sitting on the plane bound for LA:

I need to focus on that beautiful baby boy, the most beautiful boy. It is his weekend! Although I have a very strong feeling every weekend and every day is always his. He is a lucky little boy to have the world at his feet and the most amazing family to provide it for him. I am grateful to be part of it, even it is only for a weekend a few times a year.

Then, as I wrote reflecting on leaving:

When my Uber pulled up to take me to the airport, I grabbed my stuff and was slowly walking out. I said good-bye a million times, told my son I loved him over and over, and hugged him over and over again—although I still feel as if I should have given one more. I was walking back-wards slowly, still looking at them, and my son starts to cry/scream, reaching for me as I have to say goodbye. I didn't even know how to handle that situation; I just looked at him and said I would see him soon and that I loved him. Now, maybe he was crying because that's what babies do when people leave, but I felt it inside of me. I felt the sadness of saying goodbye, for him and myself. He grew inside of me for nine full months. The only comfort he knew was me, and I know that he feels that when I am near and even when I am far. We are connected in a way that no one else will ever be connected, and when I start fearing the unknown, I remember that. It becomes less fearful. I start just imagining him doing all the things I'm wondering if he is doing. I start thinking about his smile and his active spirit. My mind is at ease. Yes, I do not have the answers to my questions, but the most important question is already answered. Did he wake up loved and taken care of? Yes.

I soaked up all the time with my son that I could. If it wasn't within the allotted visitation time, though, sometimes my son's mother wasn't as receptive as I would have liked her to have been about my coming to see him. And I get why she felt that way—she was (and is) an adoptive mom who is protective of her child. She wasn't trying to keep me away because she hated me; she was likely having similar feelings as me, except in different ways. She'd often say we *all* needed to get into our own routines, the two of them included. Looking back now, I see she was right. When I had the opportunity to move to California at the time, though, I thought it would be my moment to rebuild in a season of burying feelings and being overcome by shame and powerlessness. I'd be closer to my son. I'd be put together. I'd be moving forward.

Or, at least, that was the plan.

CHAPTER SIX

♥

The Darkest Dark

In total, a handful of us from memoryBlue transferred from DC to California. Throughout the years, we turned into the magnificent seven. For Bethany and I, the road trip from DC to California was—well, let's just say it was an experience. We were both in separate cars, packed to the gills. We'd call each other on the phone to decide where we would stay the night. Once, in Reno, we stopped at a hotel sketchy enough that she had an alarm set to go outside and check on our things every hour on the hour. The next night, we stayed at Lake Tahoe. By the time we arrived in San Jose, where we'd stay, we had a plan: we wanted to live in a nice apartment, even if that meant sharing a smaller space—literally. We shared one bedroom and ordered twin-size beds online. We were such good friends that it didn't matter. I was a five-hour drive away from my son in LA—or a forty-five-minute flight.

I'd calculated it all. I'd imagined being able to attend a school event every now and then, or a game.

When I'd told my son's mother I was moving out, she seemed happy for me. Still, I'm sure she had a fear with my being closer, and she said we'd still need to stick to our three visits per year agreement. I was excited and genuinely hopeful for a fresh start: after I'd had my baby, I thought I needed to be far away because I couldn't handle being close. Then, when I was far away, I felt like I needed to be closer. Then, I was closer again—and it would turn out I was right all along.

As I wrote in my blog at the time,

> I thought moving to California would solve everything. I thought it would bring me peace to be close to my son and in a new environment. I thought this was where I belonged. I am starting to see that all I am doing is running. I am running from myself and my past. I am learning that being in California does not really mean I am close to my son. It means I am a five-hour drive away—that I can't make. I knew that coming out here, but I think in my mind I thought it would bring me peace to be closer. All it has done is create frustration that I am so close, yet so far away. I can't just jump in my car and see him, and I knew that before I moved out here. But that doesn't make it any easier.

A NEW LIFE IN CALIFORNIA

Obviously, being near my son but not able to see him hit me hard. I turned again to distracting myself, this time by going out to parties. In my experience of California, party drugs were everywhere—Molly, ecstasy, coke. You'd have thought there were pill dispensers in every apartment hallway. At first, it wasn't bad. I dabbled and went out every so often, which I thought was a reasonable amount. I still had my life, my career. Everything was fine.

Still, I slipped up every now and then. In retrospect, I clearly wasn't making the best decisions. Bethany also worked for memoryBlue, and she wanted to leave the job. It was a great company, and I loved working there—but I quit, too, right alongside her. I don't know why. Later, I regretted it and even apologized to the co-founders— the co-founders of a company I respected and that had brought me to California in the first place. The job switch wasn't a good situation for someone like me—someone with an addictive personality, who was making choices pulling me farther and farther away from my light. I was subconsciously screwing my life up because that's what I thought I deserved.

Once, when I was in LA to visit my son, Bethany and I went out the night before. We got shit-faced drunk, hitting a lot of spots in LA. My memory is in and out, but I remember staying up almost all night with one of

Bethany's friends, who was an attorney. He was trying to convince me I could get my baby back. People were always trying to convince me of that, whether they knew my story or not—and I was so drunk and sad that I just let them talk. Before I knew it, it was light outside, and we were supposed to meet my son and his mother at the park. I called my mom, frantic, asking what we should do. I wasn't a danger to anyone by any means, but I did feel awkward and down on myself. We eventually met them at the park—and, admittedly, we were hungover and miserable. I wasn't sure if my son's mother could tell or not—or even if she'd care, because she was young once, too—but I was horrified at myself. *I really screwed this up*, I said to myself. *I just miss my son so much. Am I overreacting? What's going to happen?*

Bethany only lived in California for about seven months before she missed home and wanted to move back to Minnesota. I was already seeing I was on a downward spiral and thinking I should get out of there. I knew I'd miss Bethany terribly and thought about leaving, too. I considered moving closer to my Aunt Becky again, who at this time had relocated to North Carolina. I thought I'd buy a house and fix it up. In fact, I did more than think about it—I even accepted a job in Charlotte and shipped a few boxes down. My plan was so concrete that my sister Abby even got on a plane to California to help me pack my things and drive across the country, again.

One night, I was sitting with Mark and Cate, two of my friends (who happened to be from Minnesota, too) with the most beautiful souls. We were in their hot tub shortly before the move, talking about my impending trip to Charlotte.

"What are you thinking, Hope?" Mark asked. "I don't know if this needs to be brought up or not because I'm sure you've thought about it, but what about your son?"

It hit me then: my running away was selfish because being close to my son without seeing him was breaking me to pieces. I decided to stay and hope it would get better, that somehow my proximity would turn from a problem into a solution. I had a seemingly great life, after all—at least from the outside.

Looking back, though, I think I knew the truth even then. Internally, I knew that my friends could do things recreationally that I could not. For them, it was about having fun. For me, it was about getting high. My friends' advice came from a well-intentioned place; they tried to convince me to stay—and it worked—but I still felt a little like I was throwing my life away little by little because I just couldn't stop. It was something I didn't say out loud.

When my sister arrived, instead of driving to North Carolina, we drove down the 101. It was a bonding trip; Abby and I hadn't talked much when I was pregnant, but this time, she even got to stop with me in LA and meet my son. It was a wonderful moment, but also strange. A weird piece of that visit was the jealousy I felt. When my son paid attention to my sister, I remember feeling territorial and a little annoyed that I had to share. I couldn't control the feelings in my gut.

Overall, Abby's visit was short-lived because we got into a fight again before she headed home. Still, to this day, she's the only one in my family besides my mom to ever meet him, and that's special in my heart.

Abby left, and so did Bethany. Then, a lot shifted in my life. I rented a room in a house with two chill guys who I rarely saw, and I had a lot of downtime—which, historically, wasn't a good thing for me. The months passed, and even though I was in sunny California, my life felt pretty dark.

THE MOMENT IT BECAME REAL

I thought I'd found a bright spot when a group of my friends wanted to rent a house in San Diego for Memorial Day Weekend.

Perfect! I thought. *I'll be going right through LA. I'll stop and see my son, maybe at the park!*

When I texted my son's mother to ask, though, she said I'd already seen him for my allotted time that year because she was counting the stop with my sister. It was within her rights to tell me no, but the fact that she did hit me hard. Maybe she meant it was something we had to discuss, but my mind immediately went to her trying to keep me from him.

I absolutely lost my shit. This was a turning point in my life as a birthmother: I freaked out, telling her she was going to have to explain to my son one day why she wouldn't let his mother see him. I wrote message after message, losing my mind. It was a conglomeration of everything I'd experienced: never getting my say, never even feeling like I could ask for anything, never getting to really be alone with my baby, never being allowed to stay with them when I did visit—all of it. Looking back, it was an odd reaction, like when you're having a shitty day, one person sneezes on you, and you lose it. It's not because of the sneeze, but rather it's because of all the stuff that happened before it.

Whatever the reason, I was seeing red, and I was scared. I kept flipping back to the contract in my head, thinking she had all the power and control.

In that brief moment, I came to terms with the gravity and reality of my choices. It hit me like a ton of bricks. Everything that I'd buried deep beneath the surface came to life, and it felt like I'd just placed him yesterday. Looking back, for all those years, I was like a shell of Hope walking around. I was in a fog. I intellectually knew what had happened, but maybe because of all the trauma associated with it, it never felt real. I only let the real parts come out when I was drunk or high.

After that moment, it was real all the time. That meant my self-medicating habits turned way up. I wasn't partying to have fun anymore; I was partying because I needed to in order to be okay.

After the San Diego trip fiasco, my son's mother suggested I talk to a therapist—which was a good thing, in retrospect. I got so drunk the day before my call with the therapist that I took a nap in my car before our scheduled time. By the end of my conversation with her, I'd let it all out: I told her I did bad things, but I wasn't a bad person. All I'd ever wanted was to be a part of my son's life and to be there for moments. I told her about the recurring dream I'd had of attending his gymnastic recitals or baseball games—just of being in the audience, not even talking to him. The therapist told me my desire to love and support my son was actually a good thing, that it would show him how important he was to me in the end.

I turned into a "yes woman" even more after that,

doing anything my son's mother—or anyone, for that matter—said I should do. When my work in the L.A area picked up and I was there frequently, my son's mother suggested I meet her, only without my son there. I agreed—anything to be even one degree closer to my son. Sometimes, I'd even take an Uber and go past the park they'd play in, hoping to just see him for a second. Even through the window. All in all, I had no fight left, not even to fight about the Airbnbs and how expensive they were when I'd come to town. In truth, I knew they felt extra expensive because I was spending too much of my money on things I shouldn't: coke and alcohol, mainly. It even put me in credit card debt.

The partying got to a point where I had two groups of people: my good friends who accepted me, and the men I got fucked up with. I was hanging out with men romantically who weren't good people. In fact, I became infatuated with a hot Australian rugby player who used to come around. There wasn't love there; there was attraction, and we'd get high together. I slept with his best friend, and he didn't even care. I know everybody has problems, but the people I chose to surround myself with lived within their problems. I was in a low place, going from a point of feeling like I needed to be drunk or altered to talk about my son—which brought me peace, momentarily—to a point of needing to be drunk or altered because I was trying to dull my pain, to numb myself. Two extremes, and neither good.

At work, they had a name for my multiple call-ins: "Hope-itis." I had Hope-itis a lot back then. I was still bomb-ass at my job, though. That was the excuse I constantly used to justify my behavior to myself. *I'm fine, right?* I thought. *I'm still doing great at work. How bad could it be?*

But it was pretty fucking bad. I was getting high even on weeknights, even alone. I'd lost seventy pounds. My friends had an intervention for me; I appreciated their concern—and it was earnest. I did have good people around me. One friend called me out in the mall. One friend would pull me into the hallway and have long conversations. Other friends would hold me while I cried. I had people who knew there was a problem and were super supportive. They asked me what I needed and told me they'd support me no matter what. I loved them for the offer, but I didn't love myself enough to care or accept it. *I can't do this anymore, but I can't stop, either,* I thought. *What is the point?*

Sometimes, I didn't care if I lived. I felt like all the light I had was walking around outside my body, and I wasn't allowed to touch it. See it. Smell it. Hold it. God, how I missed my boy. But I did have a little light left in me, it turns out, and I saw it clearly one night, thanks to Giana.

A TURNING POINT

It was a warm California morning, and I was sitting outside on Mark and Cate's balcony. I'd been puppy sitting their dog, Luna—the only other creature besides my brother who'd only *ever* given me unconditional love. (Maybe my friends tried, but I hid my problems from them or wasn't receptive at the time.) Luna was a comfort in my life. I loved watching her.

I'd been up all night—literally. I hadn't slept. Coke will do that to you. When Giana woke up, she came and found me on the balcony—still looking exactly like I had when she'd gone to bed hours earlier: a lot lighter than I was just a few months before, and more than a little out of it.

"What the fuck, Hope?" she said. "What are you doing?"

Giana knew me so well. I didn't have to answer her because she already knew what I was doing.

"You have so much light coming out of you right now," she said. "You have no idea how much you radiate. You do so much for so many other people, but you don't allow anyone to help you. You're allowed to feel pain when it comes to what happened—that pain is BIG and it's YOURS. And it's okay. But you're also allowed to feel light. We all see it in you, but you've got to see it for yourself."

Since my son was born, I'd had so many little funerals in my mind. A funeral for losing my son. A funeral for never having kids again. A funeral for never having a husband or a wife. A funeral for all the Christmases, all the soccer games, all the hand holding—all the *life* I just didn't see myself having. I didn't think I deserved it.

After years of this reel of minifunerals playing in my head, that one conversation with Giana flipped a switch in me.

I had *light*?

I looked out from the balcony then, cigarette smoke snaking around my head, and stared at the mountains in the distance. I saw the beauty of the landscape around me. I saw the beauty of my friend next to me, her words still electric in the air. I didn't yet see the beauty in myself, but for the first time—the *first time*—I thought it may be possible.

The minifunerals didn't stop altogether after that, and I didn't suddenly become an angel. But Giana's words helped show me that even if I didn't love myself yet, I could. That it was possible. That I had pain, but I also had light. That there was a path forward, and all I had to do was step onto it.

That small moment on the balcony changed me. It started

me on the path to forgiving myself. To seeing and loving all of me, even the broken parts. It pushed me toward a light I hadn't known existed.

It helped me find Hope.

CHAPTER SEVEN

♥

Finding the Light Again

A lot happened after that moment on the balcony: Giana and I still lived together, and we started going for walks together and reading. We'd sit in the living room and talk about our goals. My priorities started to shift. I started to spend more and more time alone doing positive things, and people even started to call me a flake. I realized it wasn't in my best interest to go to two- or three-day ragers anymore. For example, I bought tickets to a festival and only ended up going one day. I didn't stop having fun by any means, but I slowed down on the poor choices. I was trying to wean myself off and be the best version of myself. A lot of that had to do with my conversation with Giana, but a lot of it had to do with sitting with myself and looking for healthy female role models.

I realized that before I found my light, I'd compare myself

to my son's mother in unhealthy ways. Finally, I learned I didn't have to compare myself to anyone, but instead I could surround myself with role models and work toward my purpose—yes, my purpose! I now had one. I wanted to be better.

During this time, I'd often think back to one horrible memory: I'd been up partying, and my body had started twitching involuntarily. I was alone. I laid down on the floor of my bedroom in the fetal position, almost calling an ambulance. *If anything happens to me, would anybody notice?* I thought. It was a terribly scary moment, but it was also a part of finding my light again. I had to go through that darkness to realize I was worthy of having a why, of making better choices.

Giana and my very best friend Sasha encouraged me to go to more networking events, too, which I loved. There, I heard powerful, confident women tell their stories. I thought of one of my role models since I was a child, Reese Witherspoon. I used to watch *Legally Blonde* with my mom all the time, and I'd wanted to become a lawyer. I can specifically remember being hungover back in my party days and seeing a video of Reese on social media at the Glamour Women of the Year Awards. She mentioned her production company that empowered women. I started to think I could be one of those women—ambitious, strong, powerful, respected. That was and is my purpose. To get to and stay in my light during those post balcony months, I was actively trying to trick myself into happiness, waking up every morning and allowing myself to be sad for only fifteen minutes. Then, I'd tell myself I was going to be happy, and that's how I greeted the world.

At one networking event in particular, I saw an incredible speaker. The next one I attended had yet another speaker who really impacted me—and it turned out they were from the same organization. I sent them balloons and a note that said, "Hey, I saw you speak. It was great to meet you. I'd love to have coffee and learn more." I wasn't looking for a job; I was looking for mentorship.

I heard back immediately—they didn't want to mentor me; they wanted to hire me. It was perfect timing, as I was at an impasse with my current boss and needed a change. Things had started to look up: I hadn't stopped partying completely, but it had stopped ruling my life. And when I did party, it wasn't as debilitating and hardcore as it was before. I'd turned a corner and taken back control.

I also realized that in the past, I'd taken on a lot of my friends' problems as my own—which I was happy to do, because I loved them and because that's part of being a friend. They'd call me to vent about their partners, families, jobs—you name it. I, on the other hand, didn't vent often, even though my pain was deep. (Although Sasha and Sam would say differently; they've heard and helped a lot over the years!) Yes, I did say I missed my son during big moments—holidays, etc.—but it's not like I could just call up my friends on a random Tuesday and cry. Or, at least I felt like I couldn't.

Giana helped me see that historically, I had taken on too many issues—and not just with my friends. My mom has cancer? I jumped in. My sister got pregnant? I jumped in. My brother needs a caretaker? I jumped in. A yes person, always. Until that moment, I'd never allowed myself to ask for help because I didn't think I deserved it. I'd never thought I could say no or that I needed time.

Did I need to hit the party drugs so hard? No. But maybe I *did* need to hit rock bottom to help me see the only way to grow was up.

FAKING IT TILL I MADE IT

Greeting the world as a happy person didn't turn me into a happy person overnight. I've always struggled with depression. After my son, it got worse, and my desire to deal with it shrunk. All told, it took five years of faking it until it clicked—maybe more. Slowly, I climbed out of my hole. I excelled at my new job. I continued going to events. I listened to podcasts. I read a ton of books, including rereading *Succulent Wild Woman* by Sark—the book I'd read years before, on the trip to Hawaii my son's mother gifted me after I graduated college.

My son's mother had gotten me affirmation cards, too, and I carried them in my car. One card said, "I'm safe. It is only change," and the other said, "I'm beautiful, and everyone loves me." I read those cards over and over. At first it was almost laughable—I didn't believe either of those things for one second. After I said them enough times, though, the phrases started to seep into my being. I began to believe in the law of attraction. I'd spent too long telling myself, *I placed my son for adoption. I'm a drug addict. I don't deserve happiness. This pain is what has been coming to me.* And, lo and behold, that's what happened. When I changed my language, I started to change my life.

It's not like I snapped my fingers and was suddenly fixed, though. Another traumatic experience happened when I was living with Giana, and it pushed me right back down. Even in my time of light, I had another month of making terrible decisions before I crawled out of it again.

In fact, sometimes I crave the darkness when I get stressed, and I have to fight like hell. While writing this book, I visited friends and chose to leave the social event a few days early because I knew I may be presented with situations where I might not be able to say no. That was huge for me. When that feeling strikes, I have to tell myself I am safe, successful, and have a great life; even if those things might not feel true, I have to speak them into existence. Then, I have to take actions in line with them.

Yes, I saw the light. Yes, I felt happy for the first time in a long time. Still, I had—and still do, to this day—slipups, and I go back into that dark place. I think that's okay. My accepting my light wasn't about finding a "cure" for what was ailing me; it was about accepting what had happened and being committed to moving forward, wholeheartedly loving myself along the way.

My light wasn't me saying, "I stopped drinking excessively and doing coke, so now I'm healed." What I did stop doing was being miserable on the inside. I stopped seeing myself as irrevocably broken. Today, I'm still broken, but I see those cracks as opportunities. When I think about my light, I think about my potential—about all the things I *can* do, not all I have to do just to make it by.

FULL OF LIGHT, TODAY

Today, in my light, I know my boundaries. I know what I need, and I'm vocal about it. There's nothing wrong with that. I know when to say what I'm feeling. Those affirmation cards that used to be in my car are on my desk, reminding me. I have a vision board, reminding me. I have an alarm that goes off every day at 11:11, saying,

"Would you follow yourself for success with what you achieved today?" It, too, reminds me—I have ownership of my life, today and every day.

In the past, I used to think, *I'm a drug addict. I don't deserve happiness.* Now, I think, *It's okay to feel sad,* and *I am a good person.* I say those things all the time—in the mirror in the bathroom, driving—anywhere and everywhere. If I don't take those little steps, I can feel a negativity coming over me. I can feel a big fight coming with those I love. To ward it off, I make an effort to show gratitude. If I think, *My son is no longer with me,* I will tell myself, *Yes, something that pushed me down happened. My son is not with me—that's true. But he is alive, and he is healthy.*

It's not just my language that's changed; it's my outlook. When I was twitching on my bedroom floor? I survived that. I am grateful for just waking up in the morning, so I can maybe reach at least one person who may be struggling. To inspire them.

Before I found my light, I looked at life like a series of transactions. I was living for the next high, the next weekend, the next guy to hang out with, the next city. After I stopped faking being happy and actually allowed myself to feel that, I realized I had a choice all along. That's sometimes the hardest realization to come by—that you have a choice. I discovered I didn't *have* to make bad choices to feel better—that having pride in myself felt pretty damn good, too. I finally knew that my making a bad choice every now and then didn't make me a bad person.

When I think about who I am today and what I have gone through to get here, I am proud. That's a newer feeling for me. I wake up focusing on my light and my potential. I am confident that the person I was four years ago—in the middle of a shit storm—would never believe she is the person I am today. How quickly we can all change!

In the past, I was filled with such terrible feelings—heartache, depression, anger. Then, I'd feel guilty for having those feelings in the first place because I put myself in every situation that instigated them. I didn't think I had the right to vent about something I'd been a party to, because I was the one who placed my son for adoption in the first place. When I realized it wasn't complaining but rather acknowledging that my pain was real and valid, doors opened—including the door to love.

CHAPTER EIGHT

♥

In London and In Love

The night I met Boujemaa, something in me sparked. I'd come to London for work and had plans to travel around with one of my friends, Erin, while abroad, hitting Paris and Amsterdam. I had been thinking of moving to London for almost a year at that point, looking for a fresh start. This trip was for work, and I was loving it. We'd gone out the night before, and she was insistent that we head out again to see her friend's band play. She kept telling me they played cool music and it would be a great show.

I was tired, hungover—and frankly, didn't care. Finally, because it was her good friend, I agreed—on one condition: they had to have food, preferably chicken strips. The plan was to eat, have one glass of wine, watch the band, and come home to sleep.

That didn't happen. I wanted to ask Erin if I could take her keys and just go home. I wasn't feeling it.

First, the bar didn't have food. But as I walked in and saw Boujemaa on the stage, it didn't matter. He was singing in a different language—which I'd later learn was Arabic—and I swear the world stopped around us.

I turned to my friend—who had in no way been trying to set us up—and gasped, "Oh my God. Who is this man? I've got to know him."

"He's singing about you," she said. Erin, who understood the language, said he was singing about the beautiful woman brought to him—me! The next thing I knew, he'd stopped mid-set to come over and talk to me. At first, it was awkward. I was talking to others around me, and he just stood there—weird, but in an endearing way. I wondered if he was going to say anything. Then, he asked me if I'd take a video of the band, Gnawa UK, on his iPad.

Aren't you supposed to be playing right now? I wondered. *What is happening?*

I said yes, of course I'd record. At the end of their set, I was at the bar. He walked up to me again—big, fringy leather jacket and all, hair in dreads. Very rock star.

"Can I buy you a drink?" he asked.

"Sure, let's both get one," I replied. He didn't want one, but he did want to step outside to smoke. I joined him, and I remember there was so much staring. He at me, me at him. We couldn't stop looking at each other, couldn't break our gaze. One of us was out of cigarettes, so we started to walk across the street to the gas station. He stopped me in the parking lot, turned me toward him, and blurted out, "I have five kids."

"I don't care," I said, immediately.

There was a bus right in front of us, blocking the view of the venue. We didn't want our mutual friend to see us kissing, so we stepped behind the bus.

"I have to kiss you," I said.

"And I have to kiss you," he said.

And we did.

It felt like a movie. We talked all night—I told him about my son, about my life. He told me about his kids, about his life. From that night on, I've never wanted to leave his side. I knew I'd wanted to move to London long before, but I'd just come on this trip to have fun. Meeting Boujemaa changed the kind of fun I was going to have. It just clicked.

A LOVE STORY

The next day, Erin and I got on a train in London, and I missed him right away. *Should I call him?* I wondered. *What if he's not actually interested? Like just another one of those musician types? Just another hookup?*

Right as I was about to ask Erin what she thought I should do, Boujemaa called. He wanted to make sure I was navigating the train okay. I'd been gone all of twenty minutes. The next day, we were at Erin's, getting ready to go back to Boujemaa's for a Gnawa ceremony he was hosting. Erin was taking forever! I kept telling her to hurry up, and she told me to relax. When we arrived, it was the most spiritual event I'd ever been to—the music, the vibe. I remember I wanted to kiss Boujemaa the whole time, but couldn't until the ceremony was over.

The next night, Erin and I missed our flights. We had events to attend, but I never went back to her place to get my things. She actually had to bring me my suitcase from her house *to a wedding* because I never went back to her house after that. Boujemaa didn't want me to leave, and I didn't want to leave, either. *What am I going to do?* I wondered. *I live in another country.* Still, I'd known from the moment I met him that things were going to change. I'd wanted to be in London, anyway, so it all felt meant to be from the start.

It was ironic because I'd never been a fan of relationships, and I hadn't truly had a healthy one since high school. In between, I'd just bounced around and focused on doing my own thing as an independent woman. Sometimes, nice guys would come into my life, and I'd self-destruct those relationships. My friends would ask why I wouldn't give these guys a chance, and my answer was simple: I didn't want to. I loved my son, my friends, and my family so much that I didn't think I had enough love to give. I saw myself as a burden that I didn't want to bring into any nice guy's life. *Why would they want that?* I wondered. *Why would they want me?* That was my philosophy—until the moment I met Boujemaa. I suddenly felt an earth-shattering connection, and, for once, I felt like I deserved it. It was new for me. I immediately told my friends that I loved this man. Because of my track record of being so anti-romantic about love, they believed me—even though it was all so sudden.

Erin and I went to Paris for a few days and then Amsterdam, and the entire time I was thinking of who I'd left behind in London. I canceled my flight back to America and extended my time an extra two days, but eventually the time came for me to return. It was heartbreaking. I had a life and a job in California. Although I told Boujemaa I was coming back and just needed a couple of weeks to get my affairs in order, he wasn't sure. We both had little fears in our heads, I think, wondering if we'd be able to make it work.

We did. During that time, we talked on the phone every day, sometimes falling asleep with the other person on the line. I went back after two and a half weeks, and I went to meet him near a coffee shop. I lugged my suitcases around the London streets with my phone pressed to my ear, asking him where he was. Suddenly, I saw him and he saw me. He started sprinting toward me, both of us in tears. It was a beautiful moment.

That visit, we spent a lot of time in the park, where Boujemaa loves to play his instrument, the Guembri, which looks like a three-stringed guitar. He's Muslim and Moroccan, and it was around the time of Ramadan. I was fascinated by the experience—the fasting, the ceremonies, the beauty. Everything about Boujemaa felt like music to me, and it still does.

On top of spending time with Boujemaa, I loved my time in London—grinding for my job and soaking it in. I remember telling him I was a strong, independent woman, and I liked it that way. I told him my career was important to me. There were times I'd have to walk out of

Ramadan dinners to take calls, and the hours were (and are) long and sometimes inconvenient. It was a sort of reverse culture shock for him, but I was up-front straight out of the gate. I knew then—and I know now—that sometimes personal growth comes before a relationship, for both women and men, and that's not a bad thing.

After spending more time there, it was official. I knew in my heart what my next step was and what I needed to do to be happy: it was time to move to London. Career-wise, the opportunity to move to London with my current company was no longer available, so I took a couple of months off to get acclimated postmove. My old CRO had become the president of my current company, Eightfold. ai, so I used the time to settle in while I was waiting for them to get the budget to hire me.

When it came to London, I wasn't sure how my move would impact my son. I also knew that, while I loved California and all my friends there, I simply couldn't be my best self when I was there. Being close to my son yet apart was breaking me. I knew the move was the right decision—and it has been. Now, I'm able to visit him as often as I can.

A SAFE PLACE

Boujemaa and I fit so well together because he is an

addition to my life. I didn't need anyone to complete me. He has always made me feel complete just how I am. So, when he asked me to marry him, I couldn't say yes fast enough. I would have married him the day I met him. So, when we went to the mall to look at rings after I'd moved there, we found some we loved. The next day, we went back and tried to find the jewelry store. We walked around and around, and we couldn't find it anywhere— but we did find another store. There, we found an even better (and cheaper) ring, and he bought it. Boujemaa has been married before, but he'd never bought a diamond. He's a minimalist—except when it comes to instruments and costumes! It was a special moment for him to be able to give me what I wanted. When we left the store, we both turned and laughed—the original store was right next door!

In the Uber on the way home, I told him I wanted to go to Spain for the weekend. What was the point of living in London if we couldn't enjoy the area? He said no, and I was angry. Lo and behold, he had an engagement party planned for that Friday.

I knew the rings were in a bag in the back of the Prius we were riding in.

"Can I just see it?" I asked. He relented.

"Can I put it on?"

He put it on me, and I never took it off.

Yes, we got engaged in a Prius!

MOVING ON UP

After the engagement party, a lot happened for me pro-
fessionally. I vividly remember being at the dentist when
Boujemaa and I got the call. It was Eightfold.ai! They'd
gotten the budget. I told them I'd need to wait until after
I returned from an already-scheduled trip to Mykonos,
Greece, with my mom—and both of those decisions were
some of the best I've ever made. I learned a lot about my
mom on that trip—about how losing my son hurt her, too.
About her side of the story. I let go of a lot of anger then.
As I wrote on my blog:

> I feel so sad that I let myself go through all of this mostly
> alone for many years. I had my family and friends, but I
> didn't like to share my emotions. Very few times did I let
> it bubble up and come out, and neither did she [my mom].
> What if we had been there for each other the way we are
> now during those years? What if I had let myself realize that
> my mom was feeling all the pain I was? She hurt. I hurt. It
> wasn't until I saw those tears in her eyes in Mykonos did I
> realize that she needed me as much as I needed her.

Career-wise, getting on board with Eightfold.ai was one of the best decisions I've ever made. Today, my job gives me a lot of purpose. It's a startup, so I have a lot of responsibility and wear a lot of different hats. It's brought out the "hustle and organize" side of me, and it's helped me grow as a person. In this role, I'm in front of executives at the largest banks in the world. As a woman, I'm sitting at those tables. Our mission statement reads, "In Buddhist philosophy, the Eightfold Path guides each person to wisdom and nirvana. We are inspired by this ideal, and through our work, we wish to empower each individual to pursue the career path of their choosing, gaining the knowledge they need to achieve their goals and aspirations." I'm behind that 100 percent on a deeply human level. Being in the tech industry, and AI geniuses, they could have gone a million different ways, but the company chose to be mission-driven. Today, I wake up every day and believe in what I'm doing. I'm willing to get up early and work late. It fuels me. I've been presented with many opportunities not typical of a twenty-seven-year-old, and those didn't just fall into my lap. I've worked hard to get here, switching my mindset both in my personal and professional life. I'm a businesswoman today, and I'm proud as hell.

RELATIONSHIP ADJUSTMENTS

There's a lot of passion in my relationship with Boujemaa, and one of the biggest adjustments for me has been being a plus one. I'm not used to being with someone and having to consult on decisions. I also tend to keep my feelings to myself, so I've had to work hard to not get angry or upset if Boujemaa doesn't understand or acknowledge that I'm sad or upset. Usually, it's because I haven't told him. When that happens, I have to step back and check-in with myself. *You are in a safe place*, I tell myself. *It's okay to talk about how you feel.*

There have also been times he didn't communicate well with me, and we'd hit a wall. At the end of the day, merging cultures is hard. Our first language being different has added a whole different layer to our communication. I've also had to work to recognize some of my own tendencies. For example, I've had to learn that I can't control things. My therapist explained that women who place children for adoption take an authoritative place in their own lives whenever possible because they often feel like they didn't have choices or control before. And, when they can't, they can have huge reactions. This was eye-opening to me, and when I look around, I can see it manifesting in my life. I have to be conscious of how I show up in this relationship for Boujemaa, and he has to be conscious of how he shows up for me. We're both flawed in our own ways, but we're a team.

THE MEN IN MY LIFE

I have images in my head of the men in my life—Bouje-maa and my son—meeting. In this dream, usually we're together on the ocean. For some reason, when I think of this moment, we're always by the sea. Boujemaa is from Morocco, and he always talks about the sea. When we moved into our new house, we hung a photo that says "Take me to the sea" in our bedroom; it was another full-circle moment.

My son's mother was supportive of my move, as she's always wanted me to be happy. She's always been like a supportive parent to me, even offering to connect me with people she knew in the area. I'm sure she was a little confused at first, though. We've had some tough conversations around whether or not Boujemaa could meet my son—something he fiercely wants to do—and time will tell.

During a recent visit with my son, I told him all about London. About Amsterdam. About Paris. I told him I'd send him postcards from everywhere I go and would always carry him with me. I told him about Boujemaa—who my son's mother said I should refer to as my "friend" instead of my fiancée. She said it caused confusion. I said I understood but really didn't. While I'm improving, there are still some things I don't feel like I have the luxury of pushing back on.

Later during that same visit, she did say it would likely be okay if Boujemaa met us at the park during one visit—not the step I was hoping for, but a step in the right direction. Still, when I got home to London after that visit, I sobbed. Boujemaa aches to meet my son, putting his pictures all over the house next to photos of his own children. He talks about him all the time. He loves him—he doesn't even know him, but he loves him because he's a part of me.

His kids love my son, too. They buy him little gifts at the market out of the goodness of their hearts, not because we told them to. My stepdaughter and I recently had a conversation about him. She wanted to know details and said she wished I'd kept him because she wanted to be his big sister all the time. This made me smile, but it was also like a punch in the stomach.

The thought of Boujemaa and my stepkids not ever properly being in my son's life is a thought that haunts me, still. I mourn it a little every day, but I still have hope.

CONSIDERING PARENTHOOD, AGAIN

Boujemaa has five children, and one of them lives in our house on the weekends. When he first told me about his kids, I was unfazed. I had a stepdad come into my life when I was young, and he was one of the most important people in my life. I'd seen it work. I knew it was all about love. It didn't scare me. It still doesn't.

The first time I met Boujemaa's son Sully in person, though, I was incredibly nervous. *Will I be able to look him in the eye and not see my son?* I wondered. I came from a background where I wasn't sure if I ever wanted kids, and I was worried how I'd explain to my son that ultimately I ended up with five stepkids. I had so many questions: *How can I make sure my son knows he was always enough for me? Will he hate me someday?*

All these thoughts and more ran through my mind before I met Sully. I didn't know if I was capable of being a good bonus mom. I didn't know if I could be who he needed me to be. I'd finally gotten myself to a place of healing; Would this open old wounds? It was a pivotal moment for me: I was either going to sink or swim. It was going to work, or the relationship likely wasn't going to last.

When I met Sully, though, my worries melted away. I instantly knew I could love this kid. I instantly knew that my mom's statement that I wouldn't be a good mother was false. I instantly thought, *I can do this.*

And I have done it. I've made a lot of choices in my life to ensure I can accommodate them. We moved to a bigger house. I try not to travel as much for work. I try to keep things consistent, keep a house full of love. It's been an awakening, and one I'm proud of. When I got a card from my stepson last Christmas that read, "Best Step-mom Ever," I broke down. Because I *am* a good stepmom, dammit. And I'd be a good mom, too.

Sometimes, it is stressful figuring out where my place is. I want to join the PTA to help my stepkids. Am I allowed to do that? I found myself right away getting too involved, and that started to cause problems with their mother. I wanted to be as involved as I could, but I learned to take a step back and find that line. At the end of the day, I understand both sides. I don't want to take anybody's place. I understand what it feels like.

Now, Boujemaa and I are considering having a baby of our own—not at this exact moment, but maybe in the future. I know that if we choose to have a baby, it will be a beautiful and joyous experience.

I obviously still have a fear that my son will hate me if I make that choice, but I've resolved myself to one fact: I have faith in that no matter what, he is my son. I am his birthmother. Nobody will ever have the bond we have—and if we hit a rough spot, we'll get through it. There have been moments when I've felt like something is wrong from states or even an ocean away, and I've texted his mom only to learn my son is sick. We are one. Our hearts beat together.

If he gets pissed at me one day when he's older, if he yells at me, I may deserve that—and even if I don't, I'll honor those emotions. And we'll be okay, always. This knowledge and trust in our relationship has been an awakening that's brought incredible peace into my life.

Looking back, I can pinpoint moments in my life where my self-sabotage spiked. My drinking put me in a lot of scary situations where I didn't always have control or feel safe. I've had lots of sexual interactions with men before having my son and after, and not many of them sober (before Boujemaa). I used sex like I used drugs—to get high, to take my mind off the pain. If I couldn't feel love, I wanted to feel *something*.

Don't get me wrong—I am a firm believer that people are entitled to sleep with whoever they want, however often they want. Sex with a stranger? Go for it! Live your life. It's not bad that I was having sex with all these people—it's bad that I was making that decision not out of joy and love for my own body, but out of sadness. Out of self-destruction. It took finding a *true* love to see that. It took finding myself.

Ultimately, I now know I spent almost five years trying to fill a void that didn't need to be filled. The person I am now—writing this book, being a stepmom, a good partner, traveling to see my family, spending time with my son, trying to build a social following to help other people—the person I was before could never have done this. Not in a million years. Now, not only am I doing them, but I'm doing them well. I needed to find myself, live for myself, and build a positive life. Here I am: new city, new love, new career, new Hope.

Conclusion

I think of my son every day. I have fantasies of him growing up, calling to tell me he misses me and wants to come
hang out. Fantasies of seeing him over Facetime and
scrolling through his Instagram feed. Fantasies of him
and Boujemaa at the beach, splashing in the waves.

Those are what-if's, and I can't let them consume me.
Here are the facts: I miss my son. Nothing that happened
was ever his fault—not one little bit. At the end of the day,
my son's mom is the best mom in the world for him. She's
doing something I felt I couldn't do at the moment, and
she's doing a wonderful job. I feel lucky the universe gave
her to my son and me. I can see it in the way she looks at
him, the way she cares for him—they've got a connection.
She makes sacrifices for him every day, making sure he
can go to the best schools and have his best life. And she'll

always have my back, no matter what. Does that mean we'll agree about everything all the time? No—but we'll get through it just like we've gotten this far: together.

Recently, she sent me a text explaining she didn't want my son to meet Boujemaa on our next visit. I flashed back to the text message about San Diego when she said I couldn't see my son. It was the hardest moment of my entire life. My lowest point, so far. The moment it all became real.

But this time, my reaction was different. Instead of freaking out, I simply said, "I don't like it, but I respect you. So, I respect it." That is phenomenal growth, knowing how I would have handled that situation before. I spoke up for my own feelings while remaining calm. And it's all true, too—I truly do respect my son's mother. I know she's got her own set of considerations she's dealing with. We all do.

In fact, looking back, I realize a lot of people have been scared and scarred in this ordeal besides me. My mom— who actually visited me in London while I was writing this book—was scared that her child was pregnant and could get hurt. And I know she misses my son, too. We've since reconciled from those troubled days. Yes, there will always be fire in our relationship, but there will also always be love. I needed her at twenty-one, and I need her now.

My son's mom has had moments of fear, too, no doubt. Just like I'm scared that I could lose rights to my son, she's probably scared he will wake up one day and say he wants to be with his birthmother. I don't believe for one second that she ever intentionally made me feel like a vessel; she was doing what she thought was best for my son. We all were.

At the end of the day, my son's father was a villain in my life for some time. But when I look back, he was scared, too. We were kids. Maybe it wasn't handled the right way, but I understand now where the fear came from. For him, though, he wasn't carrying the child. He didn't face any real repercussions. He was just using words that weren't attached to anything. I'll never forget how he treated me, but I don't hold any hate in my heart toward him.

EVERYBODY'S GOT A STORY

Everybody's got a story about adoption, whether it's theirs or that of someone they know. My mom had a friend from high school who was adopted; he didn't find out until he needed a blood transfusion and the paperwork didn't match. He spent his whole life feeling like he didn't fit, like something was missing. None of us wanted that for my son.

Professionals agree. My hope is this book can help open minds in the adoption world and prove that open adoptions can be successful, even if they're messy at times.

As Sharon Roszia, M.S., says, "Open adoption is about the needs of a child so that they don't have to lose a family to gain permanency—it makes adoption about addition, not subtraction. It does not diminish pain, sadness, concern, or disappointment. It requires the adults to make a healthy, trusting, honest relationship in order to benefit the child."

I agree with Sharon—it's all about the welfare of the child. Not knowing who you are is hard enough as you grow up without the added component of not knowing your birthparents. I say this from an honest place because on some level, I understand that emptiness of not fitting very well, and I don't want that for any child. As a birthmother, sometimes I'll be in a conversation where people are talking about their children, and I don't know how to respond. I have a child, but he's not with me. What do I say? Am I allowed to have a voice?

I vividly remember a conversation with my stepson and his friends. One of them asked if I had any kids, and I didn't know how to answer.

"Yes," Sully said for me. I shook my head, defeated.

"Why wouldn't you talk about it? Why is that a bad thing?" he asked.

He was right. Yes, I've found the light. But sometimes, I need someone to hold my hand and keep me there, even if it's my fourteen-year-old stepson who is young enough to be unjaded by the world and wise enough to see that my answer actually doesn't make me a burden to anyone. It makes me a person—a person with a story, just like everyone else.

Today, I know that I don't have it all figured out, but I'm definitely worthy of goodness. I've had the tools around me the whole time but didn't realize it. We are all like that to some degree. We know what it takes to get healthy, but we don't do it. We know we should walk away from a bad relationship or friendship, but it's easier to stay. Sometimes, when you can't see past your own problems, changing your mindset is the only way to move past those blocks and believe that you are worthy. The affirmation cards that I kept in my car? They were there for years before I used them. Years! The confidence that I could, in fact, make a change for the better? I think it was always there, too, just cemented in shame and heartache.

I've shared with you the story of my redemption, and my

pain. Yours will look different. As I mentioned before we started this journey, pain is pain. It all hurts, and it's all valid. I wish I wouldn't have gone through those dark times alone. I can't go back now, but maybe I can help you feel not so alone. If we can lift each other up one at a time, we'll feel a collective rising. Look around you: maybe the tools you need to pull yourself through a tough time are within your reach right now, like mine were. You just need to feel your own light enough to find them.

Trust me, it's in there. I don't even have to know you, and I see it.

P.S. I love you, Son.

Afterword

Every day I replay different scenarios over in my head—different topics, different conversations. A lot of them include my son. I have thoughts like, *What would this situation had been like if...?* or, *What if I had held him when he was born?*

The list goes on.

At the core of all of my thoughts are the things I would say to him if I could. Here are the things I want my son to know, forever and always:

1. You are always on my mind.
2. **This is not your fault.**
3. I have loved you since the moment I felt you in my tummy.

4. My pain is not your burden.
5. **I am always with you.**
6. I hear you.
7. I will always be your mom.
8. Everything is as it should be.
9. You bring joy to my life.
10. You've taught me true love.
11. You are my guiding light.
12. **You were and always will be enough.**
13. You did nothing wrong.
14. Your existence is worshipped.
15. I will always be here for you.
16. I will never leave you.
17. Your life matters.
18. You are important.
19. You are going to do amazing things in this world.
20. **We will always be connected.**

—HOPEY

Acknowledgments

To my son: I thank you for existing every day. I thank you for your love and your curiosity. There is not a day that goes by where I don't wonder how you are doing, how you are feeling, and what you are thinking about. You are the light of my life. You are my reason for being. When I think about what I want in life, I see you.

To my son's mom: You are more than my son's mom. You are my friend and my village. I thank you for your unconditional love for our son—and for me. I knew the first time I saw you that you were it, and I've never wavered on that thought. I love you.

To the love of my life, Boujemaa: You came into my life when I needed you the most. I needed to see myself through your eyes. You gave me another reason to live.

You showed me what life could be like. It's not always easy, and it's far from perfect, but I love you so much. I am thankful for you every day.

To my stepkids: I love you. Thank you for letting me be your bonus mom. Life with you is fun.

To Amber, my person: You walk this life with me every day. Every day. I knew I could count on you then, and I know I can count on you now. You are the best mom in the world, and I hope to be half the mom you are to your girls and Ledger! You gave me the gift of nieces, and those little chicken nuggets are the light we all need! I love you all.

To my mom: Even in our darkest of times, I know you always love me and I hope you know I will always love you. Thank you for doing the best you could and walking through this with me. Let's keep moving forward with love and light.

To Maury: Our silent saving grace. You have shaped who I have become and made my life better. I always know I can count on you. Always. Even when I piss you off, I know you will be there. Everything you have ever done for me is not lost on me. You are a gift to the world. Don't you ever forget it.

To Riley, Abby, and Nick: You give me life. You always

have and you always will. Thank you for seeing me and loving me.

To my family: Dads, sisters, brothers, aunts, uncles, grandparents, cousins, and beyond—I'll never know the exact words to say, but I thank you for standing by me and helping me through the darkest times in my life. I thank you for helping me off the floor. For bringing my nieces and nephews into this world. I thank you for understanding why some of you were not told till long after my son was born. I thank you for loving me!

To my beautiful friends (and your families): Wow. Where would I be without our balcony conversations, late-night talks, pool days, kicks in the ass, pushes in the right direction, pep talks, support? I love you all. I thank you all. From the bottom of my heart, thank you.

And **to Jessica Burdg:** How do you do it? Thank you for working with me on this important journey. This is as much your success as it is mine. Your ability to understand my feelings and innermost personal thoughts and then put them into words is incredible and beautiful.

I could go on and on, but I think there is a limit to these things. So I'll stop now. :)

—HOPEY

About the Author

After placing her newborn son for adoption in 2013, **HOPE O BAKER** struggled with depression, addiction, and overcoming the stigma that surrounds birthmothers. In her first book, *Finding Hope: A Birthmother's Journey Into the Light*, she shares her story of a successful, open adoption—and all the heartache and light that came along the way. Hope is a passionate advocate for those on all sides of adoption. You can find her online at HopeOBaker.com or follow her on Instagram at @HopeOBaker. Hope visits her son regularly, and she currently lives with her loving partner and her wonderful stepkids.